The Land of Maybe

Following the natural cycle of the year, *The Land of Maybe* captures the essence of 'slow life' on the 18 remote, mysterious, wind-buffeted islands which make up the Faroes in the North Atlantic, where just 50,000 people share Viking roots and a language that is unlike any other in Scandinavia.

We follow the arrival of the migratory birds, the over-wintering of the sheep and the way food is gathered and eaten in tune with the seasons.

This is not a travelogue, but a deeper exploration of how 'to be' in a tough landscape; a study of a close-knit society and a way of life that represents continuity and a deep connection to the past. *The Land of Maybe* offers both a refuge from the freneticism of modern life, and also lessons about where we come from and how we may find a balance in our lives.

'These dispatches from the wind- and salt-blown islands at 62 degrees north offer delicious escapism. A beautiful evocation of landscape and nature, it is, above all, a portrait of a community which maintains a deep connection with its past.'

FINANCIAL TIMES

'The natural world is the crucible of Ecott's observing: the hares, ravens and seabirds, the extreme weather, and the isolation of the self-reliant islanders all spin a fascinating narrative that has all the hallmarks of becoming a classic of modern nature writing.'

ROBERT TWIGGER

The Land of Maybe

A Faroe Islands Year

Tim Ecott

First published in 2020 by Short Books,
an imprint of Octopus Publishing Group Ltd
Carmelite House, 50 Victoria Embankment
London, EC4Y 0DZ
www.octopusbooks.co.uk
www.shortbooks.co.uk

An Hachette UK Company
www.hachette.co.uk

This paperback edition published in 2021

10 9 8 7 6

A CIP catalogue record for this book is
available from the British Library.

ISBN 978-1-78072-518-5

Printed and bound in Great Britain by Clays Ltd, Elcograf S.p.A

This FSC® label means that materials used for the
product have been responsibly sourced

Cover design © Two Associates

All the lives this place
Has had, I have. I eat
My history day by day.
Bird, butterfly, and flower
pass through the seasons of
my flesh. I dine and thrive
on offal and old stone,
and am combined within
the story of the ground.

'History'
Wendell Berry

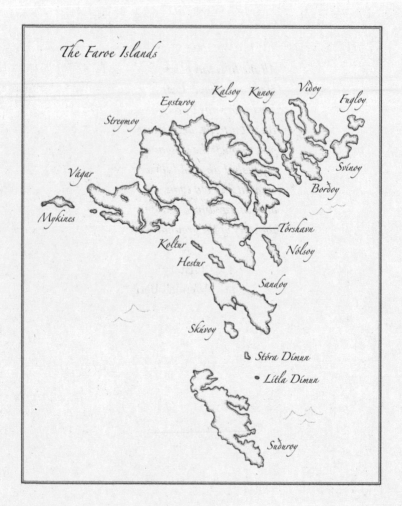

The Faroe Islands

Kalsoy Kunoy Viðoy Fugloy

Eysturoy

Streymoy

Svínoy

Vágar

Borðoy

Mykines

Tórshavn

Koltur

Nólsoy

Hestur

Sandoy

Skúvoy

Stóra Dímun

Lítla Dímun

Suðuroy

Contents

Illustrations by Jessica Ecott

1

62° North

The high cliffs of Mykines are a jagged wall facing into an endless ocean. On this long August night, the quick northern light gives the sky a fish belly shine. It is time for the men on the rocky ledges more than a hundred metres below me to be hauled up with their catch.

Lying on my belly and crawling to the edge, I peer over the drop to see that it's Esbern who is first to reappear from the killing grounds. He leans back, walking up the sheer wall as the rope gang pull steadily on the line attached to his waist harness. One hand on the rope for balance, he holds two live gannet chicks in the other. Sharp beaks gape wide above his grip on their long speckled necks.

Jóhannus meets him as he reaches the top, seizing one of the gannets as other men gather around. The bird slowly extends its wings wide like an angel. 'You will have this one,' he says, passing me his knife. I balk, unprepared for the moment, mumbling something about not knowing what to do. Jóhannus looks me directly in the eye. 'I got it for you,' he says calmly, pushing the chick towards me. I grasp the silent creature firmly by the neck, conscious that it is almost the size of a goose, at least in length if not in weight, but certainly twice as big as a large chicken. The extended wings span at least a metre. Doubts crowd in on me. I have not even seen how they kill the birds. A dozen pairs of eyes are on me, and the other men must wonder why I, the *onglendingur*, should get one of the first gannets.

The chick is now quiescent, and I avoid looking it in the eye. It feels heavy, but calm in my grip, incapable of knowing what is happening. Jóhannus tells me to bend the gannet's head down using the beak as a lever with one hand and, with the other, push the knife into the side of its head just behind the eye. Then, I must cut decisively around the arching neck. For a split second, I consider saying no, and handing the chick back. Apart from being unsure of whether it's the right thing to do, I am nervous of getting it wrong. I am also conscious that Jóhannus is doing me an honour. I fear the embarrassment of appearing feeble and unmanly, but I am equally worried I will muck it up, maim the bird or let the knife slip and end up injuring myself. In a split second, with these equally unpalatable options racing through my mind, I resolve to do it. Sure enough, I underestimate how difficult it is to push the knife into the bird's head. 'Try again,' Jóhannus says calmly. This time I press hard and pull the blade across the neck, as though I am slicing the top off an onion. There is a moment of resistance, and then a sensation like the release of air if you pop a tennis ball. There is no gush of blood, no violent quivering or fluttering from the chick, just a sudden irrevocable limpness as the elegant wings fall slack along the length of its body. I have the strong sensation of a switch being turned off, and a very real sense of the movement from quick, to dead. I hope that my queasiness and ineptitude have gone unnoticed.

Jóhannus takes the lifeless gannet from me and puts it on the pile with the other dead birds. The tally for the night is more than five hundred, from a colony of around 5000 adults. All around me the other men are sitting on the grass, breaking out their picnic food. Those who had been down on the ledges in the hours of darkness look like coal miners. The effect is magnified by their hard hats and head torches, but the real resemblance is in their grimy faces. Some have blood on their hands where they have been pecked, and many have ripped trousers, but they are all smeared in black streaks, exactly as if they have been down a mine. It is a combination of oil from the feathers of the gannet chicks, and gunk and guano from moving among the nests along the ledges. And, through the grime, their features look worn and drained by sleeplessness, and they have the dog-tired look of men who have been concentrating on a tough physical task. They are also calm and cheerful. Evald, a teenager, tells me he killed around twenty gannets and that he has been waiting for this night for years, wanting to follow his father down the cliffs. His grandfather is one of the handful of people who live on Mykines all year round, and he has been coming here every summer for as long as he can remember. Evald admits he was a little scared at first, but says that the excitement of what he was doing soon wiped away the fear. 'My mother doesn't want me to do it,' he says, 'but she understands that I have to. My little brother is very jealous. But he is only eight, and too young to climb.'

The Faroes bulge out of the Atlantic halfway between Shetland and Iceland. The wind blows fierce and the mountains merge with the sky in sudden descending mists. Brooding hunched headlands and iron-grey cliffs drenched in spray and spume are pounded by deep North Atlantic swells. Killing animals and birds for food is still part of everyday life for many people here. It is not the clinical abstract industrial process it has become for so many of us in larger-scale societies. Slaughtering is done at close quarters, animals despatched humanely with a knife to be eaten at home and shared among family and friends. They are not afraid of blood and guts. Their reality can be brutal, and quite literally visceral. If it is a symptom of their Viking heritage, I cannot say.

The 62nd parallel runs across these eighteen islands, all remnants of the Thulean plateau, a half-forgotten geological area that makes up part of Ulster, the Inner Hebrides and some portions of Iceland, stretching all the way across the ocean to Greenland. Once Norwegian, but now a self-governing part of the Kingdom of Denmark, the islands were long held Viking territory. Even before that, over 1200 years ago, they were a Celtic outpost, and those cultures and languages are linked together here as strongly as the basaltic shelves that provide the surface rock rising above the Atlantic waves. And then there is that wind. It blows stronger than anywhere else in Europe, and speeds of a 100kph have been recorded in

eight months of the year. In December 2016, a new record
– 283kph (176mph) – was set at Norðradalsskarð, in the
mountains just a little way north of the capital Tórshavn.
That's a higher wind speed than Hurricane Katrina.

All that weather can't be ignored. It has driven much
of what it means to be Faroese. In 1943, a British soldier
stationed here wrote a pamphlet explaining that 'Kanska
is the Faroese word for "maybe" and it is the most used
word on the islands. They are ruled under a despotism –
the not so benevolent despotism of the weather. Five times
as much rain as the wettest part of the British Isles – five
hundred times as much wind as the windiest part. Maybe
we'll go fishing tomorrow – maybe we'll try and do a bit
of haymaking – maybe we'll get married. All and every
one of these things is conditional – you see maybe it will
be too wet to bother with the hay and a rough sea makes
it impossible to go fishing or get married….'

Repeated visits to the islands mean leaving my wife
Jessica and our children behind in England. It is part
of a pattern of restlessness, perhaps born of a childhood disrupted by the constant prospect of moving
abroad because of my father's army career. As an adult,
I continued the pattern and when my own daughter was
a baby I plotted and schemed to leave London and move
to some other small islands, in the Indian Ocean. I was
younger then, and the lusty tropical heat and warm water
where I could go scuba diving as often as I wanted had an
obvious appeal. It's possible I am searching for something
that only islands seem to offer. I deny it, although Jessica
claims that men find islands appealing because they hold

the promise of private kingdoms, imaginary holdfasts to escape from the problems we cannot face at home. They are the lair of the Bond villain and the home of Prospero, sanctuaries where power can be wielded absolutely and the wide sea forms the ultimate moat.

Jessica is sanguine about my repeated absences. She went with me while I pursued that tropical fantasy. Moving from London to paradise for two years when our daughter was a baby seemed a reasonable escape from a hemmed-in, frenetic and urban northern-hemisphere life. I was drawn there by blue water and white sand, by chittering fruit bats and flying fish, by gentle turtles and giant millipedes that oozed harmless black ink when you held them in the palm of your hand. I thirsted for immersion in that shimmering naked blue sea. But, after a time, I learned that the idyllic-seeming island was a restless place, a reservoir of deep discontent for incomers and natives alike. The fruit bats and the turtles never lost their charm, but the searing tropical sun eventually illuminated a basic truth. Islands do not automatically confer sanctuary and can easily become seductive prisons. I gradually came to see that the steamy, brightly lit sensual charm of the Indian Ocean had turned into something gaudy, brash and, ultimately, insubstantial. There was turmoil and discontent just beneath the surface. The islanders dreamed of escaping to somewhere bigger, and the foreigners who washed up onshore were usually running away from something, or someone. Most frequently they were running away from themselves.

Faroes has little in common with a tropical paradise,

except perhaps for relative isolation and a small population. My equatorial home had palm trees and no sheep, while this one has more sheep than people – and because of the scouring Atlantic winds, barely any trees at all. When visitors say the landscape is harsh, barren, stark or bleak, I bristle. It may seem like all of these things, but for me it holds immeasurable beauty. There is comfort in these basalt crags rising from a mirrored sea that is dark as a raven's feather. Bare mountains, riven by deep fissures, roll away to the horizon in un-numbered shades of green and gold.

The ancient traditions here have much in common with the way people in Ireland or the Outer Hebrides lived three or four generations and longer, ago. Even so, life is changing fast and modern development inevitable. But for now many of the old ways remain, and they go beyond some kind of quaint folk museum exhibit. Many of the customs to do with sheep, seabirds and farming have parallels with how people survived on St Kilda until the early twentieth century. Those islands share not just steep cliffs, but also a history of settlement by anchorites, invasions by Norsemen and a reliance on puffins, gannets and fulmars in order to survive the winter. Life without the strong cooperation of your neighbours was impossible. In Faroes, that culture survives in the way men gather together in the autumn to collect their sheep and go into the mountains to shoot hares and out to sea to catch fulmars with nets. Fishing still occupies much of the workforce, and the perils of braving the North Atlantic remain a real and present danger. A man needs to be dependable to earn respect.

Things have changed, of course, and the modern world is very present. An increasing network of bridges and sub-sea tunnels means you no longer rely on a boat to get between many of the islands. Faroese people enjoy the fastest internet speeds in Europe, and mobile-phone coverage reaches every nook and cranny of the archipelago. Like us all, they now communicate obsessively and constantly online, and around forty per cent of the population lives in or close to the capital, Tórshavn. Populations in smaller villages and islands are dwindling. But, in spite of all this progress, a significant number of people are holding tenaciously onto their traditions. In the villages, Christianity still holds sway, and Sunday is a quiet day. Shepherding and fowling, pilot whaling and fishing, and eating a unique form of air-dried meat remain central to the islanders' lives. In the capital, it is now possible, though expensive, to live a life similar to anywhere else in urbanised Europe, and buy all of your food in the supermarket. My friends in the villages reject this tactic and sometimes mockingly refer to the 'city folk' of Tórshavn, people who no longer know how to skin a sheep or shoot a hare.

The weather here is no less changeable than it ever was. Impatient clouds deposit rain 300 days a year. The downpour fills the gorges, making the rock face shine, and along stony stream beds the seeping, trickling flow gathers into waterfalls that spring from the hillsides and run towards the sea. Glistening silver torrents burst through the mossy flanks of the fjords, like pulled cotton threads from the lining of a rich brocade coat.

Just a decade ago, on my first journey to Faroes, my plane was diverted because of low-lying fog at Vágar airport. There were only about forty passengers on board, and we ended up staying overnight in eastern Iceland. We all became friendly with the crew and stayed up late playing cards in the small hotel bar near Egilsstaðir airport. The friendliness and stoic acceptance of the Faroese travellers struck me deeply, especially as it was a Bank Holiday weekend and most of them were only going home for a few days. Losing twenty-four hours of their short holiday didn't seem to be upsetting them unduly, and no one complained. The next day we returned to the airport and, after clearing security, were told that the fog was still bad in Faroes, and we all had to go back to the hotel. We did this again, and then again, three times in all before lunchtime. It reminded me of an old film called *The V.I.P.s* starring Richard Burton, Maggie Smith and Rod Taylor. The whole plot was built around a departure lounge at Heathrow airport and the relationships of the passengers stranded by fog. On the fourth trip to the airport, the Faroese pilot (with whom we were all on first-name terms by now) came to us and said, 'I've been on the phone to Vágar, and they say the clouds are still very low. But we could just go and see if things get better. What do you think?' A show of hands revealed that everyone trusted his judgement, and we duly took off. After circling for more than an hour, he finally came over the intercom on board and said, 'I think we can make it.' And so we did. I remember that the airport was almost deserted, and a single customs official ignored us all as we trooped through the arrivals hall. In spite of our enforced camaraderie, there were no effusive goodbyes as everyone melted away into the mist-cloaked car park, as if we'd all been on a school outing and would see one another again soon.

Since then, the national airline has modernised its fleet and extended the runway at the airport, which was originally built by the British during the Second World War. They say the location was chosen because it was hemmed in by mountains and would be less vulnerable to enemy bombing. It was also one of the few places flat enough to lay a runway, and near to a significant port and a big lake suitable for flying boats. Recently, the national airline, Atlantic Airways, was the first in Europe to develop a highly specialised computerised system that would allow its aircraft to use an instrument-only approach with much more precise parameters than anywhere else. The system has cut cancellations and delays due to weather dramatically and is the envy of many other airports in northern Europe. It's typical of Faroese adaptability, and I continue to be stunned by their endlessly practical attitude to solving problems.

The mutability of the weather here has shaped not just the land, but the way people look at the world. It is why they band together and still value community. The persistent wind means they have no trees on the high ground and precious few at sea level. The only animals that thrive are the hardy sheep that remain central to their lives. Surviving in that severe physical environment is why people customarily ate pilot whales and seabirds and why they still seem immune to some of the worst excesses of modern life. Seventy years ago, the Scottish author Eric Linklater described the Faroese as having 'a primitive virtue to which they add the graces of a native culture – and they appear,' he said, 'to have escaped the vulgarity and inertia of civilisation'.

I realise that I too find an escape here, certainly from the vulgarity that creeps into life in a bigger place. This is somewhere that enforces mutual respect. You can't be rude to anyone easily, as in this small population of just over 50,000 people that person may well be a relative, and if not, you will certainly meet them again. There are other qualities that I recognise from Ireland. Here, people love to talk, and they have a highly developed sense of humour. Arrogance and any sense of social superiority have no chance of survival.

Seventeen of the eighteen islands are inhabited, although one of them accommodates just a single married couple. Another has been inhabited by the same family for over 200 years. One, almost impossible to land on from a boat, is just for sheep, and then there are the dozens of skerries and islets, a jigsaw of lava fragments that spread east to west no more than 75km, and a little more than 110km north to south. Travelling by car means negoti-ating roads that wind around 250 mountains, many of them almost 900 metres high. Aside from the cliffs and the looming mountains, the sparkling streams and gushing falls, the islands are dominated by sheep. Hefted to the land, precisely numbered and individually accounted for, they outnumber the human inhabitants by half again. The sheep are significant because they have been the key to survival here, in a place where little vegetable matter other than grass and dwarf shrubs will grow. And the name Faroes (until recently spelled Færoes in English) probably derives from the Old Norse for sheep *fær* + islands *oyar*. In Faroese, the country is properly called Føroyar – pronounced *furr:ee – ar*.

There are sheep beside the road, in paddocks in the capital, on the mountains and in the valleys and along the shelving precipices of the cliffs, where on vertiginous slopes and dissolving scree they teeter, scrabble and climb. Sometimes you even meet them in the car park at the airport. The sheep and their bleating cry are as much the music of these green mountains as the shrill call of the oystercatchers. Those sounds are as welcoming to me as the smell of hand-cut hay spread with a pitchfork, or the taste of blackening mutton hung in a wooden shed to dry and then fermented in the wind that howls off a winter-dark fjord.

Ravens I

Vágar, early spring

There are ravens in the gorge. They have built their nest in a wall that the rain makes as shiny as their own beaks. This pile of sticks and twigs, moss and feathers, rope ends, clumps of wool and other nameless scraps has been woven into an untidy bowl. Dried and pale like old bleached bones, it forms a loose tottering thing, wedged tight against the back wall of that miniature cave. The nest sits in an uneven sloping niche just a metre deep and about twice as wide. But this is a safe house, with enough of an overhang to keep off the rain, as well as the almost constant slick of moisture that runs down from the top of the cliff, forming a dripping veil between the nest and the outside world. The fall from the niche is twenty-five metres, to where sunless seawater slaps and sucks against the base of the rockface. The water laps with a tinkling echo, and sometimes a north-easterly wind scrapes across the walls of the ravine in a hard whistle.

Down in the gorge, the air is chilled by rock which sees no sun, winter or summer. North-west of the ravens' nest, the sound glows pink in the longest summer evenings, as the barely setting orb tracks across the narrows, softening the shape of the hills on either side of the water. Even then, the cleft stays unlit, shaded by the folding land.

The sea channel is named Vestmannasund, and it flows between two of Faroes' biggest islands. The ravens and I are on Vágar, and look out across the water to the long straggling coast of the next-door neighbour, Streymoy. There are countless gorges on these coasts, many of them deeper and more dramatic than the place where the birds are nested. To reach my ravens, you need to walk along a farm track away from the main coast road and through a sheep gate. A kilometre or so further on, the track stops abruptly at a sheep pen, and to find the gorge you walk through it or around it to follow the sloping coastline on foot for a considerable way.

My friend Jóhannus (the gannet catcher) is one of the owners of this section of outfield, and on a damp day he showed me the nest. He's a shepherd and a qualified marine engineer, a rock climber and a mountain guide. He loves hunting, rarely eats a vegetable and prefers the local *Slupp* beer to any foreign import. Above all, he's a proud defender of Faroese traditions. Strongly built, with thick light-brown hair that sticks up like a brush, he has an irreverent sense of humour in five languages, but with his immensely powerful arms and hands he can kill a sheep and totally butcher the carcase in less than twenty minutes. Jóhannus has just turned thirty, and is always resolutely cheerful, though he's happiest in the mountains where he springs along without seeming to expend any effort, no matter how sheer the climb. We had gone to look for a missing sheep, spotted somewhere on the rocks below the outfield by a boat cruising up the fjord. The skipper said the animal had clearly fallen and might be injured, and Jóhannus carried a coil of climbing rope to allow him to make a cliff rescue. As always, he also had his knife with him in case the animal needed slaughtering where it lay. But the directions from the boat had been vague, and we trudged up and down for more than an hour, unable to find anywhere that matched the sailor's description, and there was no sign of the sheep.

It was on the way back north that he made a detour to show me the nook where the ravens had laid their eggs. Ravens are not loved here, and many people still believe that they prey on newborn lambs. In a country named after sheep, it's no surprise that farmers shoot them. Ornithologists say that the raven takes only carrion, or occasionally other small birds, but many shepherds claim that a gang of young ravens will attack a weak newborn lamb, especially if the mother sheep is preoccupied, perhaps giving birth to its twin. Ravens were once so unloved that, between 1742 and 1881, all Faroes men between the ages of fifteen and fifty had to pay an annual 'beak tax'. One beak, from either a raven or a white-tailed sea-eagle, had to be produced to the local sheriff each year. If neither of these birds had been caught, then the man could also offer up two beaks from crows or greater black-backed gulls. The men of the capital, Tórshavn, were exempt, on the grounds that they did not own land in the outfield. In the districts, fines were collected from those who failed to kill predatory birds, money that was used for the upkeep of buildings in town, and to build a bridge over the east bay, which became known as the *Næbbetoldsbroen* (Beak-tax-bridge). At the beginning of the annual parliamentary assembly on St Olav's Day, the beaks were ceremoniously burned on a flat rock called the Crow's Stone near to the parliament.

The reason given for the introduction of the beak tax was that predatory birds seemed to be increasing in number, and people believed they were depleting the numbers of puffins and guillemots, which were important foodstuffs. In fact, the eighteenth-century beak tax was just a reintroduction of an ancient tradition common across Scandinavia in the Dark Ages. In 1673, the Danish pastor, Lucas Debes, author of the first book ever written about Faroes, recorded that every man 'able to roweth a boat' was required to hand over one raven's beak annually, 'and he that hath none must pay a Raven-fine, that is one *skinn*, which makes two pence half-penny.' Ravens, science now proves, have a very wide-ranging diet. Northern-hemisphere birds have been found to eat carrion, including sheep and cattle, but also dead seals, hares, rabbits, voles, rats and mice. They also eat fresh berries, limpets, beetles, birds' eggs, worms, moths, crabs, mussels and seaweed. And like many birds in the world today, they have also been found with plastic in their stomachs.

Jóhannus thinks it's funny, or at least perplexing, that I return to the nest most days, and sometimes more than once a day, to check on the chicks. He knows how often I go because it's his pasture, and out of respect, I always call to ask him if I can visit. In Faroes, unlike many parts of Scandinavia, there is no legal 'right to roam' on private land. Going to see the nest site is a privilege. It feels like a sacred spot for me, and the birds convey magic too. Perhaps the gorge is what the Celts called a 'thin place' where the earthly world and the afterlife are within touching distance of one another. The raven's spirit captures something of the true north.

It was ravens that Flóki, the Viking adventurer and famed boat builder, took onboard his ship when he set out west-wards to become the first man to settle in Iceland. The last leg of his voyage was from Faroes, and it's said he had three ravens – 'the blue-feathered carrion birds' – with him, possibly captured in Shetland. After some time at sea (according to the twelfth-century *Landnámabók*, the old Icelandic 'Book of Settlements'), Flóki released the first bird, which flew 'from the stern', heading back in the direction of Faroes. Later, the second bird was released and after a short circular flight, returned to the boat. The third and final raven flew off out of sight, and Flóki headed in the same direction, always believing that the birds would know the way to the nearest piece of land. It was then that he found Iceland, and ever afterwards was nicknamed 'Raven-Flóki'.

I saw ravens as a boy in Ireland, high up in the Mountains of Mourne, and I watched them play with the wind. There were sheep there too, and just like Faroes, the heights were bare treeless slopes that up close revealed myriad tiny specks of colour; lilac harebells, eyebright and saxifrage that lit up the seemingly empty green land. The mountains lay right behind the small house where my grandparents lived, and they are my first and strongest memories of the outdoors. They imprinted me with the charm of rain and fast cloud, of high land and long views, and the strong cold smell of the wind off the sea.

2

Westernmost

They say that Mykines people talk loudly because of the sea. The island's only village, Mykinesbygd, is set well above the ocean, but when a stiff south-westerly blows, the Atlantic roars like booming thunder into the tiny harbour at the foot of the cliffs. It swamps the double breakwater and paints it white with spume. Then it inundates the rough-hewn jetty, kicking up a wall of spray, pure and delicate as a sunlit snow flurry high against the sky. The waves have cracked into fragments, temporarily separated but desperate to be rejoined. The sea now bubbles and froths across the harbour as foam. Cunningly and quietly, it slides up the foot of the steep concrete staircase leading to the village path above. Seconds later, the water withdraws like a tongue, disappearing swiftly under the rolling arc of the next run of breakers with a lisping whistle. The little harbour is a natural opening in the sheer southern edge of the island, a gloomy steep-sided cleft where guillemots and kittiwakes look down onto the waves from narrow ledges twenty metres high. The boulders that form a small inhospitable beach rasp and cough as they scour the base of the cliff, rubbing away the rock a little bit more with each rolling wave. If they can't attack the village from above, they will undermine it from below. The endless, often furious Atlantic surrounds the high sheer sides of the island, and it seems as though it can reach up and over the cliffs, merging with the clouds and the penetrating descending mist which covers Mykines like a finely woven shawl.

The village lies in a valley, nestling close to Toltnabrekka, the river that springs up from the high ground in the middle of the island. The river forms a wet border between the outfields of Heimangjógv on its northern side, and Líðarhagi to the south. It's the main water supply for the village, snaking down from a great wide moor that lies below the high rocky ridge at Oddarnir and the high point of Knúkur, almost 600 metres above sea level. East of that sharp grey seam in the land, the island divides again: dropping suddenly hundreds of metres into two deep valleys, Kálvadalur and Borgardalur, both massive natural amphitheatres where more than a thousand sheep live wild from the day they are born until the late autumn when they will be rounded up and driven on foot by men and dogs back to the village. Then it will be time for the serious business of sexing, sorting and slaughtering.

The island is shaped like an upside-down gravy boat, and at the south-western tip there is a 'handle' formed by the islet of Mykineshólmur. Surrounded by high cliffs, it has few safe landing places for boats. It's only about five kilometres from the eastern cliffs of Mykines to the western edge of the much bigger island of Vágar, but the closest points are impenetrable, with no safe, nor convenient harbours or roads nearby. The practicable route by sea from Vágar is from the port of Sørvágur, about nineteen kilometres from the western tip of Mykines. The summer ferry runs from here, at the neck of a long thin strait. The entrance to Mykines harbour is narrow and easily becomes treacherous. In the days when the parliament, or *Ting*, met once a year on the rocky headland at Tórshavn, the men of Mykines were always allowed to speak first, so that they could set off early to row back home on the first suitable tide.

Mykinesbygd sits in the bottom south-west corner of the island proper, nestled in a dale which offers some, but not much, shelter from the north wind. It has fewer than fifty houses, many of them still turf-roofed, and mostly still made of wood. The size and shape of the village has changed little in the last century, although it now has its own electricity generator and a helipad. There is a neatly white-washed church, and an untidy graveyard, a schoolhouse with no children to sit in it and a couple of cafés that only open for the summer. There's no restaurant or bar, although a few of the houses intermittently accommodate paying guests. The tourists come for summer day trips, to visit the bird cliffs and to spot nesting puffins. In winter, few people stay over for the season, and the daily ferry from Sørvágur stops running from the end of August until May. Sailings in May can be extremely sporadic, depending on the wind. Katrina Johannesen remembers one winter, before the government helicopter service began, when the supply boat couldn't reach Mykines for more than seventy days in a row. 'But,' she says quietly, 'I love it here in winter. It's a special place and I can't imagine being anywhere else.'

Katrina's husband Esbern is the man who carried the live gannets up the cliffs. He knows all of the habits of the birds here, and he keeps a pet raven called Munnin, after Odin's messenger bird. He found it with an injured wing, and he feeds it slivers of fresh meat while he tries to teach it to talk. Every Viking knows that Odin had two ravens, Munnin, meaning 'thought', and Hugin, meaning 'mind' or 'will'. Each morning they were set loose in the world of Midgard, and quickly returned to whisper what they had seen in Odin's ear. Munnin lives in a caged enclosure, tacked onto Esbern's chicken coop. Pullets scuttle in and out of their adjoining shelter, casting a wary glance at the black bird.

I met Esbern years ago, on my first visit to Mykines, when he was herding sheep out on the *hólm*, the islet, about 800 metres long, and separated from Mykines proper by a narrow chasm, a sea-cut gorge less than sixty metres wide, today spanned by a metal-and-plank footbridge. Above a beard of spun gold and copper he has clear skin and piercing eyes that shift from grey to blue like the Mykines sky. Esbern is always on the move, always busy with some practical task. He manages the ferry landings and helicopter arrivals and maintains the island generator. He's been known to dig trenches for the mobile-phone company's cable network and he owns land where he keeps a considerable number of Mykines sheep. When I arrive on the ferry, he's on the jetty in a thickly knitted Faroese sweater that seems as much a part of him as the wool on one of his rams. Single-handedly he's loading supplies onto the metal hoist that pulls heavy items up to Fjørudalsnev, the promontory above the jetty where he keeps his old boat. There is fruit juice, cooking oil, potatoes, cartons of milk and bottles of beer. One of the items on the boat is a new washing machine for Oskar, one of the ten people who stay on the island for the whole winter. I help him manoeuvre the supplies onto the metal trolley. We climb more than a hundred steep concrete steps beside the metal hawser that will pull all of the freight to the top. Once there, Esbern starts the motorised winch that hauls the metal hoist up the ramp. He says the washing machine will go on the little trailer he tows behind his quad-bike. As I move to help lift the stoutly packaged machine, he brushes me aside. In one swift movement, he wraps his arms around the washing machine and lifts it onto the trailer. Through the plastic wrapping, I notice that the box carries a printed warning: *Heavy, 80kg.*

It helps to be strong if you live on Mykines. In Esbern's snug wood-panelled sitting room, there is a large ram's head on the wall, stuffed and mounted with an impressive pair of horns showing several years' growth. Faroese rams are normally not kept alive for more than two years, as they become too large and difficult to handle. But sometimes, a ram will escape the annual roundup and find sanctuary on the cliffs. Such a ram is called *vargur*, a maverick, which may well lead the other sheep astray and make them impossible to catch. Esbern says this ram was probably around five or six years old when he found it, and there is something distinctly feral about its appearance. The horns have grown into a third spiral that descends well below the animal's jawline and halfway down its solidly muscular neck. It has an imperious look, with a white and flossy fleece, more like a silky wizard's beard than normal sheep's wool, although out on the cliffs, when alive, I suspect it was coarser. Esbern found the big ram on the steep slopes of southern Mykines and was able to sneak up on it while it was dozing. He grabbed it with his bare hands and wrestled it under control. The head stares out from the wall near to the flat-screen television. Close by, hanging from the ceiling, there is a stuffed gannet, with wings outstretched, and various other birds on the window sills and bookcases; a peregrine, a tufted owl, a white-tailed sea-eagle and some guillemots. There is also a merlin, the only falcon that breeds in Faroes. Many of the others are vagrant birds blown in on a storm.

At the beginning of spring, I feel like I have been

blown here too. I am staying in the little house next to Katrina's café below the schoolhouse. It's a traditional wooden building with a pair of gable-end bedrooms at the top of the steep staircase that divides the house into two neat halves. The roof slopes acutely above my head; it's more like being in a tent than a bedroom. When the wind blows the eaves thrum like a drum, and the whole house creaks. Waking in the darkest part of the night, I feel as if I'm drifting on the ocean. It reminds me of the myth that Mykines was once a floating island, tossed around on the sea and impossible for men to land upon.

In the weak morning light, the wind throws heavy raindrops against the windowpane, giving me only a soft-focussed view of the village. It's exactly the kind of day that reminds me of being trapped in my grandparents' house on countless wet school holidays with what felt like an eternity of boredom stretching ahead. Kumlum, the high sloping ground to the east, is totally wrapped in mist and invisible. When the American explorer, Elizabeth Taylor, came here by rowing boat in 1901, she was stranded for more than three weeks, of which only three days were in passably fine weather: 'Mykines village is not a cheerful place. A cruel looking coast it has, of brown, red and ash-gray trap rock…capped and wreathed with cloud mists. The summer is cold and short, the winds are strong; potatoes barely grow, and are small and soggy; the few little patches of barley never fully ripen. But wherever the ground is drained and cleared of stones, there the grass grows thick and long, the one sweet and gracious thing in Mykines – fragrant as sweet clover and adorned with pink

catchfly, daisies and saxifrage. Good grass and puffins are
the compensations which Mother Nature bestows upon
her Mykineser children.'

The noise of the rain hitting my window is amplified
by the surrounding stillness of the village. It comes in
irregular bursts, like handfuls of fine gravel spraying onto
the glass. My fingertips make a squeaking sound as they
rub away the condensation to peer through the small
panes. I am struck again by the Irishness of the landscape
around the village. A cloak of moisture joins the air to
the land and the sea, stirring deep memories. As a child
in Ireland, where I was born, we lived in a seaside town
where the grey light and the trickling dampness of low
skies were a mirror for my mother's declining happiness.
My interest in the natural world was forged there in a
landscape dominated by shadows skittering across the
rump of an Irish mountain, and the scattered shades of
a metallic sea that clawed at rocks thick with kelp and
rough with acorn barnacles. I recall no truly hot days, just
the thick smell of damp moss and the clammy touch of
shuddering ferns that held the raindrops hours after the
sky had cleared.

Our own house looked out to sea, and my grandparents' home was at the foot of the mountain. I spent a lot of
time there, making excursions up onto the dome of Slieve
Donard or into the sepulchral pine forest that covered
the lower slopes. Inside, we sat beside a coal fire while
my grandmother knitted a succession of garments that
never seemed to get finished. Granny loved baking and
there was always a pie or a cake in the oven. My mother

didn't knit, and she avoided cooking as much as possible, but they shared a common desperation to get away from Ireland and the damp climate. Both had married soldiers, a ready made ticket to escape the Irish weather and travel the world in the dying days of empire. Even after he left the army, Mum regularly tried to persuade my father to sell our house and buy a boat in which we could sail around the world, but he was too cautious to seriously consider it. Where she saw freedom and escape, he saw danger, ironically for someone who spent most of his life as a soldier seeing action in places like Korea, Cyprus and Borneo.

Inevitably, perhaps by a sort of osmosis, I absorbed her prejudices against Atlantic weather, the steaming windows running with condensation and endless empty Sundays trapped indoors by the rain. Every winter, I suffered with bronchitis and twice almost died of pneumonia. Whenever I became ill, Mum would recite one of her mantras: 'the doctors told me you'd never be well unless you escape from this miserable damp air.' But then, as I grew older, my health improved. I began playing sport outdoors, bird-watching and mountain walking, and of necessity much of this activity took place in the rain. 'Are you really going out in this?' she would say, 'You'll catch your death.' She would pull a face when I told her the weather didn't bother me. I felt a sense of guilt, as if ignoring the rain, or even worse, enjoying it, was somehow a betrayal of her dreams. I feel it again now as I contemplate leaving my room on Mykines. She died young, and I wonder what she would have made of my desire to be here, beset by storms and far from the high culture she craved in her own life.

In the centre of the village there is no traffic noise, because there are no cars here – just a few ATVs, the sturdy six-wheeled bikes that can cope with the mud and the bog and the steep hillsides. Not even these machines can cross over onto the *hólm*, because the path down to the bridge is too narrow and steep. Because of the heavy rain, I walk that way, abandoning a plan to climb towards the eastern end of the island, which would mean cresting the high ridge in poor visibility. The objective would be to see the grand view across the water to Vágar, but today I would be lucky to see a hundred metres ahead. The wind is too strong for the ferry to come, and no helicopter is due. It's doubtful any of the villagers will want to walk to the cliffs, so it is a chance to be alone.

To reach the *hólm* you need to climb the slope to the west of the village, and pass through a gap in a dry-stone wall at the crest of the ridge. On the right, the edge of the island drops sharply over the northern cliffs, and I've been blown onto my knees up there when the wind has been up. Near to the wall is a sturdy stone plinth that shelters two marble plaques inscribed with the names of Mykines men. On the north-facing slab are those who have died on the cliffs, and on the other side, those who were lost at sea. The names are repetitive; Abrahamsen, Danielsen, Heinesen, Joensen and, prominently, Jacobsen, of whom there are eight listed between 1895 and 1987. The wreck of the *Skemmubátinum* took six Mykines men in 1895, and in 1934 nine men from the island were lost off Iceland with the *Neptun* – including three Joensens. In a population of not much more than one hundred on Mykines at the time, this would have been catastrophic, and the *Neptun* foundered after a probable collision with another Faroese boat, the *Nólsoy*, out of Tórshavn. In total, the disaster resulted in the deaths of forty-three Faroese men. Even longer ago, in April 1595, all of the men of working age on Mykines, perhaps thirty in all, died in a storm which sank more than fifty boats around the archipelago, and cost the lives of close to 300 Faroese men altogether. Similarly, in 1913, all the men from the northern village of Skarð died, causing the settlement to be abandoned. In that year, again in the northern part of the archipelago, there were a series of sinkings over several days, resulting in the deaths of twenty-five fishermen, leaving thirteen widows with thirty-four children.

In Faroes' national art gallery, there is a monumental oil painting, called *Home from the Funeral* (*Hjem fra begravelse*). It depicts mourners being rowed home to the island after a burial. I often go to visit it. Like many great paintings, it has the ability to draw you into its depths, and as you immerse yourself in the imagery, it becomes a time machine, a magic portal that transports you to the day and the place where it was painted. It is dark, both in colour and in feeling, and the weight of human loss is overpowering. The boat journey and the journey between life and death become one, and the symbolism of the ocean as a barrier and a route to oblivion is inescapable. The image is also a step backwards, to an era when life was less certain, and perhaps valued all the more for it.

The painting shows eight figures, hunched and stricken by grief in the bow of a rowing boat. Women, with faces elongated and angular, appear like wraiths, while a couple hold hands in the foreground and a young man wearing traditional Faroese clothes sits with his head bowed. From the stormy sky ahead, to the mourning shawls of the female passengers, the tones are overwhelmingly grey and black. The mourners' eyes are hidden, ghostly and overshadowed by cowl and brow, blurring the line between the living and the dead. The combination of sea and sky, the chasm between life and death and the utter soul-wrenching bleakness of the scene are emblems for the historic struggle between the Faroese islanders and the sea.

The artist Sámal Joensen-Mikines (1906–1979) was from, and of, the island. The Joensen men from the *Neptun* wreck of 1934 commemorated on the cliff-top monument are his paternal relatives, and the Abrahamsens are from his mother's side. His work is mesmerising in its ability to convey the threat and the pathos of life on Mykines. This is the westernmost part of Faroes, and it bears the brunt of everything the Atlantic can throw at it. Here, and throughout Faroes, the weather is not an abstract thing, not something which delays a picnic or stops people doing some gardening: it is the essence of the place. Mikines is revered, not just for his painting skill, but because he summarises much about what it means to be Faroese, evoking the close connection the islanders still feel with the natural elements. This relationship is something that goes hand in hand with an awareness of the impermanence of life, the threat of cliff and storm, an ever present likelihood of death. In a nation where life has been largely defined by the sea, the power of a sudden storm is not simply a romantic idea. Joensen once wrote that he didn't understand 'why people don't want to see death in its immense beauty, as they see life.' Later, in Denmark he recalled that he had been only eight when he was first asked to sing at a funeral on Mykines, and had 'gone into the room of death and placed my hand on the chest of the corpse and prayed.'

Joensen added 'Mikines' (an idiosyncratic spelling), to his name in 1931, after receiving a scholarship to Copenhagen's Royal Academy of Art. Virtually self-taught, he was first given some old tubes of oil paint when he was eighteen, by the Swedish artist William Gislander, who visited Mykines island in 1924. Later, in Tórshavn, Joensen was encouraged by William Heinesen, who would later become Faroes' most prominent novelist. Art was Joensen's ticket off the tiny island, but the umbilical cord of memory with the traditions he observed at home and with the natural cycles of the Atlantic weather were never totally broken.

Each summer, for much of his life Joensen returned to Mykines, painting numerous summer landscape scenes of the cliffs and the village. He was profoundly affected by the Atlantic colours, which he said, 'break in a wonderful way in the moist air' in Faroese light which is 'at the same time both strong and soft'. By 1931, he had begun to sign his paintings 'S.J. Mikines', and sometimes 'Joensen-Mikines'. At the peak of his powers, he would return again and again to the subject of death, with paintings entitled *Around the sickbed* and simply, *Loss*. As well as the relatives and neighbours who died at sea, Mikines lost his father and three siblings to tuberculosis, noting that 'death is now a part of me…and in [its] shadow I painted for the first ten years of my career.' His meticulous biographer, Aðalsteinn Ingólfsson quotes the painter saying that death gave him the opportunity to capture people 'frozen at the height of their emotions, transformed into form, into art.' Fittingly, *Home from the Funeral* became the first work acquired for the Faroes National Art Collection when it began in 1948.

Alongside his taxidermied menagerie, Esbern has some Mikines oil paintings in his sitting room. Visitors to the island often ask if they can come in and look at them. Mikines painted dozens of landscapes, and other iconic images – especially of violent and bloody pilot whale drives, scenes that also reinforce the Faroese familiarity with death. Not only is he revered as a master painter, he also captures something of the mystical allure of his home island. Kristianshús, where I am sleeping, was once Mikines's painting studio, and he grew up in Oskar Joensen's house – 'Innistova' – where Esbern and I transported the washing machine. Today, Mykines remains a place that Faroese people speak of with reverence. The small village holds something timeless and reminds people of the old ways. Families share ownership of winter-empty houses and jealously apportion holiday time in them during summer. You can usually spot the people who are staying on the island overnight, as the absence of a shop means they must load the ferry and the helicopter with bags and boxes of food and basic supplies. Part of the allure of the island is that transport is still easily disrupted by the weather, and many visitors half hope they will become stranded by wind or storm. A visit to Mykines still holds an elemental uncertainty which goes deep to the soul and acts as an antidote to the predictability and sameness of the modern world.

In the village, Faroese greylag geese have hatched their eggs and parade around the narrow streets with their goslings in tow. Officially a smaller, hardier sub-species of the common European variety, they are one of the oldest breeds of domestic birds, probably arriving in the islands with the Norsemen. One pair stays close to the river with ten chicks, and whenever I pass too close they usher them off with a harsh warning hiss in my direction. It is too early for any of the wild birds to have laid their clutches yet, but out on the *hólm* the puffins have begun to mass offshore, in floating congregations. From the ridge, I watch them gather in the afternoon, usually just an hour or so before sunset in great rafts on the surface of the sea. There are thousands of the tiny birds, already in their breeding plumage with their beaks painted orange, yellow and grey as if freshly decorated for a summer party.

The weather is decidedly not summery, not even what I would call spring-like. There's a biting wind out on the high ridge where the puffin burrows pepper the slopes. They also nest on the steep cliffs of the northern side of the island. I've learned that I can sit near to the edge of the precipice and after a few minutes the birds ignore my presence, just as long as I don't move too fast or attempt to stand up. They fly very close to me, and seem to be the wrong design for aerobatics with their rounded tummies and short wings, and that curious egg-shaped head. But as they approach the clifftop, they pinpoint exactly where they want to be, and generally land swiftly, or if the wind is right, glide down gently with wings held high. Taking off directly into the breeze, they only have to extend their wings and rise as if by levitation. That serenity lasts only a second or two, as they must beat their wings furiously fast to support their chunky bodies in maintained flight. Those stubby arms can beat up to 400 times a minute, and above the sea they produce a stilted, slightly jerky motion. These are wings best shaped for maximum strength when diving underwater, where they can descend sixty metres or more, but in the air they turn the 'sea-parrots' into speeding puff-chested bullets. On land, and when bonding with their mate, the sound of the puffins' low chuckling is somehow reassuring. The male call is like the creak of an old and very heavy door being opened slowly, a sound that has been compared to a miniature chain-saw, though it always reminds me of the contented grunting of a hippopotamus. It's a quick, chesty *tchi-burrr-tchi-burrr, burr-burr, burr-burr,* ending in a final very long drawn-out *burrrrr.* Sitting on the cliffs surrounded by the sound is greatly comforting, a sign that the birds have forgotten my clumsy gigantic presence.

On the sloping bank near to the footbridge, the puffins sometimes land a little way from their own burrow. Their neighbours raise their wings and open their beaks as if they will attack. Nothing happens as long as the newcomer stoops, and slowly raises one foot off the ground and then the other in an exaggerated tiptoeing motion, inching its way to its own home. Reunited, the nesting pairs talk constantly to one another, watching each other's faces and making little bustling adjustments to their posture. Their busy, inquisitive stares draw us to them, and it's hard not to believe they are gossiping about other birds in the colony.

In late summer, the children on Mykines catch young puffins in the village during the lengthy twilight. Puffins usually leave the nest at night, in the hope of avoiding marauding gulls. In the village, they are attracted by the river, one of the ways the chicks find their way to the sea. It's a game for the children, and they do it for fun, returning the pufflings to the sea, or placing them in the river. A chick catching a ride in a stream to the sea is an *áarpisa* – the same word that is used for children who play in rivers. Sometimes a few hundred birds are caught this way. In the past, some of the travelling puffins were always kept for food – often with rhubarb jam and stuffed with a type of cake, made from sweet dough mixed with raisins. Elizabeth Taylor observed drily in 1902, that 'when only the breasts of the puffins are taken, skinned, soaked in milk for a day or two, then stewed or roasted slowly, with a brown sauce, they make a dish to be eaten with gratitude, but cooked whole with skin, feet, head and many feathers on, a puffin tastes of nothing but unrefined cod-liver oil.'

Across Faroes, as many as half a million of the birds

were taken annually, and on Mykines during a typical summer around 30,000 would be caught and eaten. Here, on just a few spring days, some puffins would be taken from their burrows by a man extending his arm into the narrow tunnel recently and laboriously dug out by those large red feet tipped with sharp claws and assisted by that stout beak. Puffins have three claws on their wide webbed feet, and the inside talon is rotated sideways so that it lies flat against the ground rather than pointing forwards like a normal toenail. It's especially useful for tunnel digging, or when male birds fight. Pulling the bird out of its burrow meant being scratched and pecked. Sometimes a special crook was used, the *lundakrókur*, to extract the puffins from the deepest recesses of their narrow tunnels. To show that the nest had been raided, it was a tradition to pluck some feathers from the victim and plant them in the ground at the entrance to the burrow to ensure no one took the other parent. Later in the season, after the egg-laying, other birds were caught on the wing by a *fleygastong*, a flexible long-handled fowling net, and it was considered ethical to spare any *sildberi* (birds with fish in their beaks) – as that was a sign they had chicks waiting at home. On Mykines, there were about fifty special spots on the cliffs – the *fleygasessur* – where a man would sit, partially hidden, to use the fowling net. Sometimes, men in Faroes would assist the puffin colonies by digging extra holes in the tough grasses at the edge of a colony. And, in spring, people only ever took a small number of birds so as to maximise the number of breeding pairs.

Very few people are taking puffins now, and I have

heard it justified only on the grounds that children need to be taught how to do it, so that the skills are not lost. People here are well aware that puffin colonies across the Atlantic have suffered a severe crash, which began around 1990. It happened with puffins as far south as Wales and France, and even in populations that had not been taken for human food for more than a century. It's highly probable that climate change and the consequent fluctuation in the availability of sand eels and pout, which the puffins rely on to feed their chicks, have been critical. Some colonies have since rebounded, while others remain critically low in numbers.

In Faroes, people have always understood that natural resources are not limitless, and much of what the islanders claimed about seabird behaviour centuries ago has now been proven by modern science. That local folk-knowledge has not, of course, stopped a general decline in several of Faroes seabird populations. Some species, like the gannets and the fulmars, are on the increase, but the auks – puffins, guillemots and razorbills – have all reduced in numbers in recent years, not just here but more widely across the northern hemisphere.

Puffins dominate the western end of Mykines, though they are also found on other parts of the island in smaller numbers. They are said to arrive here on 14th April, *Summarmáladagur*, the beginning of the summer season. In the old days, puffins were known as the 'luggage boys' of the Arctic skua, which supposedly come on the 15th. Further west, and out on the *hólm*, the gannets reign, and not far from the footbridge across the gorge there is also a small colony of Leach's storm petrels. But eastwards, in the broad sweep of land on either side of the Toltnabrekka, ground-nesting birds make use of the outfields. Following the single track out of the village, I came across the ruins of the old stone-walled infields close to the river. There is a pair of curlews here, and I always see them striding purposefully around above the sheep pens. I have tried to approach them, but they are extremely wary, even if I sit down for half an hour or more and try not to move. Their call is a sad thing, *klew-whit, klew-whit-klew-whit... kleeeooooh,* a noise somehow filled with the loneliness of flatlands thatched with pale grasses salt-burned by wind straight off the sea.

Ahead, lie the old turf grounds, which the war-time ornithologist Kenneth Williamson described as 'gloomy with banks of naked peat, and moist sunken areas bright green with sphagnum moss...the whole area dotted with the stone huts where the fuel was stored.' There is no peat cutting now, but the stone huts remain, roofless and filled with toppled stones and rotten beams. It's late morning now and I shelter against their walls from the wind and the rain blowing hard and cold from the north. The peat houses are spread out, dozens of them scattered like an abandoned village on the north side of the river where the ground is flatter. The coast is jagged on this side of the island, and halfway up the north-west flank of the Heimangjógv, a deep rift cuts into the land. A broken fence skirts the cleft and there are sheep on the wrong side of the barrier, skittish and wild-eyed at my approach. I stay away from them, not wanting to frighten them towards the cliff edge. The land slopes forcibly upwards towards the east, and I follow the curve of the coastline leading to the high ridge. There is a dizzying drop to the sea below, and the Atlantic seems more impenetrable than it did from the *hólm*. The swell is a constant rolling thing and the water has a dull sheen, like an old sapphire ring that has never been cleaned.

On the high ground, tiny birds flit up from the grass here and there, flying low and fast, and are lost against the tussocks and hillocks. The river is almost hidden in the rolling land. The sodden banks sprout long grass that overhangs clear water tinkling over roast-potato-brown boulders. There are northern wheatears close to the stream, easy-to-spot males with their rust-tinged breasts and a smart black stripe through the eye. Mykines must seem a wild place for these summer visitors, which have travelled all the way up from south of the Sahara. There are rock pipits here too, nervy little creatures streaked brown with a touch of olive green on the chest. And, always near to the rivers cutting through the moor, there are the elegant wagtails, elongated forms with dramatic black bibs beneath a bold white face topped with a neat dark cap. All of these timid little birds seem to inhabit a secret, more innocent world in this great open grassland. They come like cheering spirits to relieve my eye, which is constantly drawn to the racing clouds above, auguries of the next downpour and strengthening winds.

Higher, just below the craggy basalt ridge that divides Mykines in two, the land is strewn with boulders and small patches of standing water. From somewhere out west in the Atlantic, the wind is blowing straight up the long rise. Perched beside a large rock, I see the island stretch away in front of me, all the way to the *hólm*. It is a long narrow finger pointing out into the sea. From this far off, the water is just a shimmering tray, deceptively flat and unthreatening. But the wind reaches every part of the land, and there is no escape from its cold tongue. I cannot resist climbing to the escarpment and looking down over the sharp edge into Kálvadalur. Pockets of mist hang off the basalt walls, smoke signals warning me off the descent and turning the valley floor into a forbidden world. Esbern has pastureland here, and sheep, but it's a wild inaccessible place almost encircled by stone, with vertical walls. It is too steep to try crossing the ridge at this point, so I head south, regaining the boulder field below Knúkur.

There are two great skuas wheeling above the open moor. They have the outline of a gull, that same screechy aggressive cry and the self-important swaggering walk. One bird lands and seems to be staking out a piece of ground. In the air, the other skua heads away to the north, turning into a black fleck against the grey sky, and then cruises back in a wide arc, swooping in low and fast above its mate. They may be a pair, or just two females squabbling over a potential nesting site; it's impossible to tell. Skuas are belligerent creatures, bullying other birds, especially gulls, which they chase in the air and force into disgorging their catch before they can feed it to their young. They are also egg-stealers, and a certain proportion of their food is other birds. In Faroes, most things are on their menu; kittiwakes, oystercatchers, herring gulls, terns, guillemots, puffins and even other skuas. With a wingspan of over a metre, the skuas are stocky, heavy hunters, weighing up to two kilos. At sea, they often drown smaller birds by sitting on them and repeatedly pushing their heads under water. This pair make harsh *chark-chark* cries, and the airborne bird swoops lower and lower above the one on the ground. After a few passes, it too lands, and walks warily towards where its partner has settled in the grass. Suddenly, it runs forward and they both raise their wings high and snap at one another, leaping a foot or two in the air with beaks agape. Then, they grasp each other by a wing – at the shoulder point where it meets the body – and tumble head over heels in a furious wrestling match. Neither lets go, and I can see plucked feathers floating into the air above the duelling pair. The fighting goes on for more than a minute, and I expect one might kill the other. They roll over and over, hanging on like dogs. Then, as if by agreement, they break apart and circle each other for a few seconds, all the while jumping up and down, before both take off, flying in tight circles close to the ground. It's a synchronised dance, fast and smooth. And then they land, with one bird nestling itself into the long grass while the other stands just two or three metres away. They stay like that for more than forty minutes before the watcher takes flight. The bird in the grass has become one with the earth, its brown form almost indistinguishable from the ground.

I cross the moorland towards the southern edge of the island, passing through Ketilsheyggjur, where a hundred years ago people dug for fragments of coal. The mine scrapings are overgrown now, but a little way off there is a chair-sized boulder and an old wooden cross marking the spot where a Fokker-Friendship belonging to Icelandair crashed in 1970. Flight 704 was scheduled to fly from Reykjavik to Vágar, and the same flight had been cancelled on two previous days. On the night of 25th September, the aircraft tried again, but this time it diverted to Norway because of fog in Faroes. The next morning, the aircraft took off from Bergen with thirty passengers and four crew, but on approach to Vágar the visibility was still poor. Due to a fault with the aircraft's radar system, it came down too low as it tried to line up for an approach to Sørvágur, hitting the crest of Mykines. Heading south-eastwards, and close to the island's highest point, the plane skidded for about a hundred metres, and was only stopped from plummeting over the cliffs into the sea by the rising slope of the terrain.

Eight passengers died in the accident, and their names are inscribed on a metal marker affixed to the rock. Five others, some of them badly injured, managed to walk west, down across the rough ground to Mykines village, to summon help. Within a few hours, a rescue team from a Danish navy vessel and doctors from Tórshavn landed on Mykines's north coast. They then had to scale the cliffs at Kálvadalur in strong winds and rain to reach the crash site. Villagers then rescued the rescuers, who got lost.

The rain is hard-edged and needling cold. I shudder at the horror of lying out here on the moor, injured after a plane crash. The downpour comes and goes like a fever but there is enough daylight to press on to the top of Knúkur and peer through the mist into the east. Far below me, the open pasture shows a tracery of marks where the trickling rain courses down from the ridge wearing tracks in the turf, fine veins across a sallow cheek.

The new spring grass is still brown, not yet greening the land, and the sheep are invisible, sheltering on the steep cliffsides at the thinning eastern end of the island. Mykines fjord is ruffled with white horses, and across the water Vágar is shielded by cloud. Even nearby Tindhólmur, with its sharp high ridge, is invisible, and the wind is strongly from the south-west still. It will be another day when the ferry cannot run; this May barely half the scheduled crossings have been made. I have already been here three days longer than planned, hoping the helicopter will have a free seat when it next can land. But that is part of the island's charm. I have been stuck here before, and I know that it's unwise to make definite plans when you go to Mykines. On each visit here, I seem to gain new insight into the Faroese concept of *kanska* – maybe. *Kanska* doesn't imply that Faroese people are unreliable, or that they take a casual attitude to plans and arrangements. It is not *laissez-faire*, or even *mañana*, but rather an acceptance that human plans may be displaced by a greater power. *Kanska* acknowledges that nothing can be guaranteed on an island, or in life. More subtly, the Faroese have learned not to waste precious time fretting about whether a future event will actually happen. Even today, there is a reluctance to commit to arrangements too far ahead.

Here, in this half-deserted community, something very

ancient lives on. Family connections to those who farmed and fowled here when they could be cut off for months at a time are still present. The islanders and the natural elements live entwined.

I have tried to understand what it is that makes Mykines so powerful. It may be that it feels like a final outpost, a sentry at the westerly point of the archipelago. The landscape and the ocean setting are striking enough, but the island is so much bigger than its physical dimensions. There are other Faroese islands similar in size; both Skúvoy and Nólsoy are roughly equivalent in area – around ten square kilometres – and they too, each have only one village. They too have families who preserve their connections to the land. Each has its own distinctive physical shape and character, and its own individual rugged beauty. However, Mykines strikes visitors with a tangible spirit. The island's lure is strong. Lit by sun and viewed from the high mountaintops of Vágar, it shines against sea and sky like a floating green jewel. The eastern end, with its deep broad valleys, looks soft and plush as a velvet cushion. Close up, the steep valleys and shelving cliffs are at once majestic and terrifying, dizzying and intimidating. And always, even now, the racing tide and the buffeting winds make it resistant to any human timetable. In winter, islanders tell me they hunker down for long periods, waiting for the light to return. They do not socialise much.

At my back, there is only the ridge of Knúkur, and the long walk back down across the moor. I will go over the boulder field and past the crash site again, find the river and walk alongside until I reach the short stretch of farm track that leads back into the village. I will turn into the tempering wind and feel the hard rain on my skin. Katrina and Esbern have invited me for dinner, and we will eat roasted gannet with crispy skin served with potatoes and carrots from their land.

Ravens II

Early May

The ground is spongy as I leave the farm track and head south along the edge of the island. On this clear May morning, I can see across the water and east towards Skælingur, and behind it the mountain, Skælingsfjall, with its distinctive flat-topped ridgeline almost 800 metres high. There are small streams cutting across the land here, filled by a constant flow of rainwater that comes down from the mountains. I can jump across most of these rivulets, but when they are wider I must clamber down cautiously onto the stony river bed. Here, where the flow is stronger, it wears away the soil and the red tuff that alternates between the layers of harder basalt, leaving a stepped bed of flat polished stone where moss and stringy algae make the surface as slippery as an ice sheet. Off to my right-hand side, the ground rises to an escarpment of exposed basalt ridges a few hundred metres inland. I am heading back to the ravens, but hugging the foreshore as best I can to avoid being silhouetted against the sky. I hope to see an adult bird on the nest, but they spook easily.

The coastal gorge is hidden until you are just a few metres away from the lip, and in the night, in mist or heavy rain, it would be easy to stumble over the edge and fall to a watery death below. The water invades this narrow triangular cut in the rocky coast like an axe blow into a tree stump. A rippling carpet of brown kelp clings to a submerged ledge. It is low tide, and the shallows are clear. Long strands of matted weed rise and fall in a slow-motion swell. Momentarily on the surface, the bundled wet roots shine as if they have been oiled, and they gasp gently as the sea squeezes the air from their glossy brown tangle.

Within 200 metres of where I know the nest to be, a black shape rises high and fast into the air, a near vertical flight on rapid beating wings. Moments later, a second bird follows. It seems impossible that the adult raven pair could have heard me coming above the gentle whisper of wind and waves, but perhaps other birds have sounded the warning. There are, as ever, oystercatchers on the ground nearby and they rise too as I approach, giving out their rapid squeaking call. That breathless high-pitched impossible-to-ignore noise is, I suspect, what drives the raven parents away. It reminds me of one of those rubber dog-chew toys being squeezed rapidly. The adult ravens fly out across the sea, circling wide and high, and then head south along the coast, perhaps trying to draw my attention away from the nest. As the birds bank and turn, they show their characteristic chunky wedge of a tail. The long primary feathers on the wing-tips are like inky fingers spread against the sky.

There are other birds here. I can see little groups of eiders out on the water, all males with their showy Zorro-style masks and distinctive neck flash, a smudge of pale green, like the plush on a Victorian nursing chair that has stood by a window, deeply faded by lifetimes of sunlight. Closer to shore, a few black guillemots, more solitary than the eiders, seemingly happy to keep their distance from one another. They have prominent white patches on their folded wings, and from behind they look as if they have brake lights. And, always, there are fulmars overhead, sailing in fast from the sea on wide-spreading rigid wings. These miniature albatrosses seem to expend no effort while gliding on the wind. Despite their small size, they are magnificent long-distance fliers with boastful puffed-up breasts and quick eyes that shine like beads of polished jet against their immaculate white head feathers.

The ravens are hidden in the cleft at the furthest point from the sea. Down here, I am invisible to the birds. I must climb the sloping ground, a hundred and twenty paces from the water's edge. If the snaggle-fleeced ram has not got there first, I can lie in a grassy furrow and look down onto the nest from close quarters.

3

Island Siblings

Deep memories of the landscape seep from my Irish childhood. Whenever we returned to my grandparents' house from abroad, there was a sense of the journey finally ending when I first glimpsed the Mournes from the bend in the coast road at Downpatrick. My grandfather took me into the mountains often, and when I was five and six used to delight in hiding in the forest that covered the lower slopes. He would duck away, leaving me terrified, surrounded by the silent towering trees, only reappearing when I started to sob. My mother and he used to row about it, and even though it sparked nightmares, it never stopped me wanting to go off 'up the mountain' with him for hours at a time. Years later, I remember clearly at university being challenged by my literature professor who claimed that no one in the class knew the thrill of being frightened of the dark on a country lane with the wind blowing through the treetops. His point was that our modern, overly lit lives make it hard for us to identify with the characters in the stories of Irish writers like J.M. Synge. Notwithstanding my early terrors, at the time I lived in a cottage in a coastal hamlet with no street lighting, and often used to go out late at night to experience thoughts and sensations that had the power to conjure ghouls and nameless terrors lurking in the undergrowth. In Faroes, it was traditional to personify the dangers of going out into the mountains at night through legends about the *huldufólk*, grey wraiths that have the power to make men vanish. There is a folk belief that they are seen less often now, because they dislike electric light and have retreated into caves deep underground or in the mountains. They serve too as a metaphor for the idea that with increasing modernisation this connection to the spirit of the land is being lost.

The link between Ireland and Faroes goes deeper than their shared foundations on the rocks of the Thulean plateau. It's commonly accepted that the first settlers in Faroes were Irish monks, anchorites who sought solitude among what the ninth-century scholar Dicuil described as 'the northern islands filled with countless sheep and diverse seabirds'. The monks are presumed to have been here as early as the fourth century, bringing the original variety of sheep several hundred years before the earliest Norse settlers arrived. Vestmanna, not far from where my ravens nest, is named for the 'men from the west', the Gaels, and in certain places you find the word *papar* – the fathers – appended to a name. One of the monks was St Brendan of Confert, famous for his voyages west from Ireland and his reputed sighting of Tír na nÓg, the floating island of eternal youth. His route to North America (many believe) in the eighth century went from Ireland via the Hebrides to Faroes and Iceland. When the explorer Tim Severin replicated Brendan's voyage, he too stopped in Faroes, and recruited a local rower, Tróndur Patursson, as an extra crewman. Patursson is also an acclaimed artist, and his experiences at sea have heavily influenced his work ever since. In Donegal, at the village of Teileann, local historians believe that monks from the area went to Iceland, stopping off at Faroes 'for a rest and to put their sheep to pasture', and then continued on their way to Iceland. Some scholars even think that the name *Faeroe* may have come from the Irish *féarach* meaning 'pasture' or 'grassland'.

Staying in a small cottage in Galway in 1948, Ludwig Wittgenstein famously wrote to a friend in England that he believed he had found 'one of the last pools of darkness in Europe.' I know that part of the country, and it retains a little of the isolation and peace that drew the philosopher there. For Wittgenstein, this lack of light was essential to fostering deep thought, and beside the sea surrounded by bare hills, he found a liberating isolation that didn't provoke any kind of negative emotion. The Faroese island of Stóra Dímun, is truly one of those pools of darkness, in which sensations are magnified. There, standing at the cliff edge in the blue light of dusk, it seems as if the approaching night is a moving thing, a fast-approaching cloak that will absorb the island in another dimension.

The southern parts of the archipelago form a set of great green stepping stones rearing up from the rolling Atlantic. Draw a line due south from Tórshavn on the map and you get to Sandoy first, then Skúvoy, and then you need to veer eastwards just a fraction to catch Stóra

Dímun and Lítla Dímun. Finally, you reach Suðuroy, a much larger island, home to around 5000 people, two and a half hours by ferry from the capital. On the southern tip of Suðuroy, there is a lighthouse at Akraberg, and about five kilometres from there, swamped by ocean swells and beset by swirling currents that suck and froth around the rocks, you pass Faroes' last official solid territory, a jumble of tiny scraps of basalt barely protruding above the sea. They are the remnants of the collapsed sea-stack called Munkurin (the monk), and half a dozen other skerries known as the Flesjarnar. Keep going south for another 300 kilometres and you'll land on the Isle of Lewis in the Hebrides.

The southern Faroese islands are girt with cliffs, and the Dímuns are especially sheer. Separated by five kilometres of tempestuous Atlantic Ocean, they are two very different worlds. Dímun is Celtic, meaning 'two ridges', and neither place seems to offer anywhere to make landfall. In a rowing boat, or even a Viking longship, they would have been forbidding and hostile options, easily ignored when other islands, like much larger Suðuroy, offered numerous natural harbours and at least partially sheltered bays. From the sea, both of these towering islands are often made more mysterious yet by cloaking mists and rainclouds which eddy and shudder over them in buffeting winds. Lítla Dímun is less than a kilometre square, and 414 metres high – sixteen metres more than its bigger brother. In appearance, if not in dimensions, it has the power of Le Guin's island of Gont, 'a single mountain that lifts its peak a mile above the storm-racked

Northeast Sea, in a land famous for wizards'. I have seen no wizards, but on sunny days, I have often seen its tabletop and dizzying green slopes completely encircled by a halo of white cloud, leaving a skirt of rock visible all the way down to the water. And, in an otherwise overcast heaven, there will be a patch of blue sky immediately above Lítla, making it seem as if the island has pushed a hole through the clouds to land like a gigantic spaceship on the sea.

Most Faroese people never visit either Stóra or Lítla Dímun, but they are places that exert a powerful draw, a romantic cultural attachment inspired by the stirring events of the Faroese Saga, the oldest written account of the early history of the islands. Lítla is a forbidding place, uninhabited, and with no evidence of a permanent settlement of any kind, probably because it has no running water supply. Once the island was classified as Crown Land, but in 1852 it was sold at auction and bought as grazing land by the communities of Hvalba and Sandvík on Suðuroy, about ten kilometres away. There are sheep there, of course, owned by several dozen individuals who rally together in the autumn to sail out to catch them, keeping a constant eye on the weather in case they get marooned.

The Dímuns have always been famous for their prolific birdlife, which provided guano to fertilise the grass and made it rich grazing for the sheep. To stop them competing with their own flocks, the landowners exterminated the last few native sheep on the little island, a scrawny brown-fleeced breed similar in looks to the Soay sheep of St Kilda. I know, because one little family of three animals of the Dímun breed is preserved in the Tórshavn Natural History Museum. Shot in 1844, they are artistically mounted on a cluster of artificial boulders, and look in remarkably good condition as they peer back at visitors from their glass display case. They are rather mountain-goat-like, with narrow skulls and thin legs, wiry chocolate-brown-coated creatures whose ancestors may have come from Ireland or Scotland with the monks or early settlers. These animals were nowhere near as plump, or as shaggy, as the modern Faroes sheep which are now some kind of hybrid descended from Norwegian and Icelandic breeds brought here in the 1600s. Fresh stock was needed then after a large number of local sheep died in a run of harsh winters. The early sheep, like those in the museum showcase, also had a reputation for wildness, and the remains of a similar breed have been found in excavations dating from the pre-Viking era (pre AD 900) at Eiði on the northern end of Eysturoy. They didn't provide much meat and their fleece, more hairy than woolly, was hard to weave.

Stóra, or 'Great' Dímun, has been inhabited for a very long time, but it has just a single farmstead, occupied now by members of the same family, which has lived there for eight generations. This is the smallest inhabited island in Faroes, covering just 250 hectares, exactly the same size as London's Olympic Park. Just after the Second World War, the English ornithologist Kenneth Williamson famously described their home as 'surely one of the loneliest, and oldest farmsteads in the world'. It may be old, but it is not, I discovered, in any sense a lonely place. It is, however, dramatically isolated, and living here requires determination and skill, even with modern conveniences like electricity and the blessing of a regular government-subsidised helicopter service. The current farmer is Eva úr Dímun, and she lives there with her husband Jógvan Jón Petersen and their two children. Eva's brother Janus and his wife Erla and three younger children occupy the other half of the semi-detached farmstead. Before I first visited them, I was anxious about what kind of people could live in such an isolated spot. I soon discovered that they are sophisticated, well-informed and contented people. They work hard, and they make jokes, they are kind and they genuinely appreciate the special privilege of living here.

The farmstead is a long, sturdy stone building surrounded by byres, a milking shed and cattle stall. There is also a small schoolhouse nearby for a peripatetic teacher. Just a short walk away is the helipad, which makes life here easier than it has ever been before. Both houses are cosy, filled with music and family paintings, with big wooden tables for entertaining, and copious pegs on the wall for hanging outdoor clothing. The hall is cluttered with dozens of pairs of shoes and boots, and there seems always to be the smell of freshly baked bread. There is a constant supply of the farm's unpasteurised milk, the freshest, most flavourful and delicious I know. From the kitchens and living rooms of the farmhouses, both families can look out to sea and across the island towards Lítla Dímun. Eva is adamant that this is not a lonely place; loneliness, she says, is not an emotion connected solely with physical distance. 'You don't feel isolated when you are with the people you care about,' she says. 'I can feel lonelier on my own in Tórshavn, than I ever do here. You make choices in life, and have to decide how you want to live. We are very lucky to be here. The farm keeps us constantly busy too, and you don't sit around worrying about the things people in bigger places do.'

The farmhouses sit on a grassy plateau, a gently sloping expanse of farmland that extends in a triangle between them and the hundred-metre drop-off to the sea. Those are the lowest cliffs on the whole island, where the best path leads down to the shore for those rare occasions when a boat can put in below. From the farmhouses, on clear nights you can see the small automated lighthouse on the tip of the island flashing every five seconds. It's visible out at sea for five or six nautical miles from the point where the southern and western-facing cliffs meet. Silhouetted against the sky, there are also the battered struts of an old wooden gantry that used to support a pulley for hauling goods and livestock up and down the cliff.

Behind the farmhouses, protecting their backs from northern gales, the land rises more steeply to a long ridge, where a high plateau provides the bulk of the grazing on the island. The sharp ridgeline is just over 300 metres above the sea, but when you reach it, the island extends northwards and begins sloping gently upward again, until it reaches a height just shy of 400 metres. Meanwhile, the whole western side of Stóra Dímun is a steep wall, hazardous to sheep and men. Most of the sheep live up there on the high ground, and must be collected and herded down to the farm at shearing and slaughter time.

And, as if this terrain wasn't enough of a challenge, there is a secret spot, known as the Grønaskor, where just a few young rams are allowed to live out their first winter. It's a small area of grass on the north-western edge of the island, accessible only by following a totally exposed path, barely wide enough for a sheep. The path is a scrape in the face of the cliff, running along the crumbly rock wall like the trail of a parasitic worm on the surface of tree bark. It seems impossible that a sheep, let alone any human being, could negotiate the track, but all of the farmers who have lived on the island have had to learn to deal with it. The rams that graze at the foot of this daunting cliff get especially fat, and tasty, because the grass is so good. Janus úr Dímun told me that every year he always buys a new pair of boots with good soles before he goes to the Grønaskor. He also takes a shovel so that he can carve a bit more space for the path from the cliff face if there has been a landslip during the winter. Janus is strong and lean, a proficient competitor in traditional Faroese rowing competitions and a lusty singer of the historic ballads called *kvæði*. With such a young family, I asked him if he felt it was worth the risk. 'We won't go if it's wet,' he told me matter-of-factly. 'But you feel truly alive when you do it. And we all need that sometimes, don't we?' The farm children on Stóra Dímun are told they cannot walk the path until they are eighteen, when they can make the decision as independent adults.

The Dímun family tree is sprinkled with stories of men who have perished by falling off the cliffs while chasing sheep or catching wild birds. Less hazardously, they also grow kohlrabi and turnips, carrots and potatoes, and angelica of course, and keep chickens, ducks and geese along with a gentle milking cow and a few other cattle. Their herd of more than 500 sheep is kept in check by a pack of eight or nine sheepdogs, which set up a chorus of howling and yelping when visitors step off the helicopter and walk towards the farmhouse.

From the sea, there are only two feasible points of access to the pasture and the flat land where the farm sits: first, by the path on the cliffs on the southwestern side at Kleivin; and second, a rarely used spot on the east coast called Barmurin. This island is a place of drama. Criminals, outcasts or even women who had children 'out of wedlock' were sometimes sent to Stóra Dímun. They provided virtually unpaid labour for the farmer. Janus told me about a woman known as 'Klodda (Ragged) Liza', who came from Suðuroy, and stayed as a farm labourer for years. Another was called simply 'Øra (Crazy) Petra', but the most famous case was Annika Ísaksdóttir, whose tragic story began when her drunken father lost a game of cards and offered her hand in marriage to his opponent, the farmer on Dímun. Although she complied with the deal, she then inconveniently fell in love with one of the farmhands on the island, and supposedly got rid of her husband by poisoning him. For a few years, she and the other workers conspired to keep the authorities off the island; this they managed thanks to the difficulty of sending men up the hazardous path. Eventually, however, she was captured and taken to Tórshavn for trial. According to Lucas Debes, who came to Faroes as a priest and wrote the first book about the islands, Annika was captured when some 'nimble men of *Feroe*, by the Bailiff of the Country's order, came on the island by the East side and took the Delinquents prisoners, and who afterwards received their just punishment'.

Poor Annika's father remained an irritant to the end. It's claimed that as she was about to go to the dock, she asked him which colour dress she should wear, and he replied callously, 'It doesn't matter, you're not going to a wedding.' Convicted of murder, her hands and feet were bound and she was thrown into the harbour. Local legend has it that her long thick hair acted as a float, so she was fished out and her locks cut short. When they threw her in again, she immediately sank and drowned.

The first time I landed on Stóra Dímun, it was late spring. The fields were full of oystercatchers and there were puffins nesting on the cliffs within sight of the farm. Jógvan Jón, a tall lean man with ruddy cheeks and shining blue eyes, opened the passenger door of the helicopter and then began hauling baggage out of the rear compartment. The contents included a package of mail sent from Tórshavn and his daughter's violin, which she had left at a friend's house on a previous visit. Clear of the landing area, my suitcase was placed in a wheelbarrow and pushed towards the farmhouse by a small boy wearing a high-vis jacket and ear protectors. I later learned that he was Óla Jákup, not yet seven, and the son of Janus and Erla úr Dímun. On an autumn visit to the island during sheep slaughtering, I watched the boy cheerfully collecting freshly severed sheeps heads, and up to his elbows in still-warm entrails that his grandfather passed to him to throw into a bucket near to the carcases he was gutting. Young Óla Jákup is already a shepherd in training, and if he, or his cousins Døgg or Sproti stay on the island, they'll be the ninth generation of the family to farm here.

Janus, who is Eva's younger brother, collects family history and has a scrapbook of old photographs from his grandparents' days on the island. Like all of the family, Janus has that great aura of calm that seems to be the gift of working outdoors. The family have a shared talent for making anyone who visits the island feel like an old friend. One evening, sitting in the warm farmhouse kitchen, he showed me a collection of old photographs and a family tree explaining his ancestry on the island.

It was in 1807 when two brothers, Janus and Søren Olesen, decided to travel from Sumba, on Suðuroy, to see if they could farm the island. Finding that the land was fertile, Janus sailed to Tórshavn to arrange legal ownership of Stóra Dímun. However, when Janus returned, he had a deed for the island made out in only his name. He had also, quite suddenly, acquired a wife, a woman named Greta. Søren, feeling understandably betrayed, left the island and returned to settle in Húsavík, a hamlet on the east coast of Sandoy. Janus stayed on the island, and was eventually succeeded by his son Óla Jákup, who in turn had a son named Janus. Family lore says that he was a weak baby, and not expected to live. You needed to be especially strong to survive here. However, his mother fed him on the rich yolk of guillemot eggs and boiled-down milk, and he thrived.

Janus úr Dímun has named his own son Óla Jákup after his father, repeating a pattern established by their Olesen ancestor who got the current farm up and running. Olesen's son, Óla Jákup Jensen, was born in 1810, and died at the age of forty-nine in an accident when he was trying to lower goods produced by the farm down the cliffs to a waiting boat. The man holding the rope lost his grip upon it, and Óla Jákup became entangled and got dragged over the edge, a fatal drop of more than 120 metres. His corpse was badly mutilated in the fall onto the rocks but his son-in-law (coincidentally but confusingly also named Óla Jákup) managed to find the remains, all except for one of his little fingers. The night after he retrieved the body, he had a dream in which his father-in-law visited him and thanked him for picking him up, but told him off for not finding his missing finger. The next day, Óla Jákup went down the cliffs again to try to find it but had no luck. That night, he had another dream, in which his father-in-law thanked him for his efforts and said he wouldn't bother him again. Óla Jákup lived until he was seventy-seven, and is always referred to as the 'Old Farmer' (*Gamli Bóndin*), managing to retire and move to Sandoy where he died peacefully in 1909.

The Old Farmer's son, Janus Johannesen, was not so lucky. Janus was born in 1862, and is now known as the *Blindi Bóndin* – the 'Blind Farmer'. His oil portrait hangs in pride of place on the farmhouse living-room wall today. Sitting with his wife and baby daughter, he is bearded, dressed in a brown woollen jacket and traditional Faroese cap, and wearing blue-tinted glasses. In 1902, the

American adventurer Elizabeth Taylor stayed on Dímun for more than two weeks and described Janus as 'a big brave man...steady of nerve and quick of eye'. Janus was known as a prolific reader, and some people blamed his loss of sight on 'too many books'. In later life, in spite of being almost completely blind, Janus was able to run the farm with the help of hired hands. At the age of fifty-six (in 1918), he was holding the rope for a farmhand who had gone down on the western cliffs to destroy fulmar nests. Fulmars were a new arrival in Faroes, and the islanders believed they were displacing the guillemots on which people relied for food and eggs. The worker lost his footing, and the impetus of his fall dragged Janus towards the edge. He wouldn't let go of the rope and plummeted into the sea. Tragically, Janus was being watched by two of his young children, who had been sitting on the grass nearby while he worked. Hand in hand, they walked back to the farm to tell their mother what had happened. Neither of the bodies was ever found. The Blind Farmer's son, Óla Jákup, great-grandfather to Janus and Eva, died just a few years later, in 1924, while taking guillemot eggs, but it wasn't in a fall. He had been safely lowered down to the rocks near the landing spot where some rare visitors had arrived by boat to see the island. As he showed them the spectacularly patterned green eggs he had collected, the rope above him dislodged a rock, which fell directly onto his head, killing him instantly. Janus told me with some pride that his own grandfather, Óla Jákup's son, Janus Johannes Jensen, lived into his nineties and had died only recently in Tórshavn. Young Janus's own father,

Óla Jákup úr Dímun, is still living and returns to the island from his house in Tórshavn regularly to help on the farm, especially during sheep-slaughtering season. Eva took the farm over from him. Their respective spouses, Jógvan Jón and Erla, now play their roles in this hard-working island dynasty.

The harshness of life on Stóra Dímun at the turn of the twentieth century is eloquently captured by Taylor when she describes it as one of the three most difficult islands to access, the other two being Mykines and Fugloy. On Dímun she describes 'a gruesome kind of family... fourteen people, four with whooping cough, one with consumption, one blind, several brennivín [schnapps] addicts, several with doubtful antecedents. And indeed there were storms inside as well as out.' Dining proved a particular challenge for this 'Victorian Lady', with the kitchen and living room filled with 'crates of plucked and of unplucked guillemots and puffins, of feathers and refuse...Over the fire, in a great iron pot, fifty or sixty puffins were bubbling, when done with they were put in a wooden trough on a stool in the middle of the room, and the family, seated on benches fixed to the wall, ate dinner, a piece of black bread on the knee, a puffin in the left hand, sheath-knife in the other.'

Before the helicopters came, the farmers of Dímun were alone all winter, unless a very rare lull in the North Atlantic swells made it possible for a boat to make the crossing from Suðuroy. Today the helicopter comes three times per week, fog permitting, but the only sea traffic is the occasional sightseeing trip which calls three or four times during summer. There is no harbour here, nor even a jetty, just a small natural inlet known as á Gjónni, a cleft in the rocky skirt at the foot of the cliffs on the extreme south-western edge of the island. There is a small derelict boathouse perched on the rocks there and a slab of concrete that serves as a landing place. A tender or dinghy must ferry passengers into this cleft, and they need a firm hand to help them ashore as the sea is rarely flat calm. Once on solid ground, it's not unusual for many of them to decide that climbing the cliff path up towards the farm is too challenging an ascent. The Kleivin path is a virtually natural way up the cliff, helped here and there by some supporting planks and a couple of steel ladders braced between gaps in the route. And, because there are so few ways to get up the cliffs, it is a climb steeped in history. This part of the island is also where one of the most exciting and seminal events in the Faroese Saga took place. These are cautionary tales, a thirteenth-century rendition of tenth-century events, where legends and history are inextricably entwined, and they still inhabit the modern Faroese imagination. Even today, people name their children after characters from the Saga.

According to the legend, Havgrímur of Hov is on Suðuroy eating sheep heads beside the fire with his bondsmen, Einar the South Islander and Eldjarn Comb-Hood. Einar and Eldjarn begin to argue, because Einar says that he thinks the best and bravest men in Faroes are the two brothers, Brestir and Beinir, who each have farms on Stóra Dímun and Skúvoy. Eldjarn, however, claims that their host, Havgrímur, is the better man, and in the heat of the moment he strikes Einar. Einar retaliates with an axe blow to Eldjarn's head, killing him. As is customary, Havgrímur summons Einar to account for his actions at the *Ting* (an assembly of free men like the Icelandic *Althing*), in Tórshavn. Havgrímur is expecting compensation for the loss of Eldjarn's labour. However, Einar is supported in his defence by his relatives, the brothers Brestir and Beinir. Havgrímur loses his case, because Eldjarn had struck the first blow in the argument, but he resolves to take revenge. Ignoring the verdict of the *Ting*, Havgrímur appeals to the wealthy and ambitious landowner, Tróndur of Gøta who says he will help him attack Brestir and Beinir in return for a gift of two cows each spring and 200 ells of homespun cloth. Strangely, Tróndur is also a cousin to Brestir and Beinir, but is apparently happy to side with Havgrímur. A third man, Bjarni of Svínoy, is also enlisted in their plot, and promised a reward – this time of three cows and 300 ells of homespun.

The Faroese Saga seems complex at first, and I read it many times before I got a proper grasp on the names of the people involved. However, once the origins of the conflict are set up – and the feud established between Brestir and Beinir on one hand, and Tróndur on the other – it gets simpler. And all Faroese people know the twists and turns of this classic story, where acts of vengeance and high drama are played out by the archetypal main characters against the very real and recognisable landscape of the islands, with a few excursions to Norway and Denmark.

Knowing the Saga makes being on the islands where

these events took place a richer experience, and when, after several years of trying, I finally got the chance to go to Stóra Dímun, the landscape and the personalities of the legends sprang to life. It was here at Rakhella, at the base of the cliffs on a rocky ledge, that Brestir and Beinir had to face an attack by three boats steered by their enemies, Havgrímur, Tróndur and Bjarni of Svínoy. Brestir and Beinir had been out sailing with their young sons, Sigmundur and Thorir, possibly checking up on their sheep which they grazed on neighbouring Lítla Dímun. As they get home to Stóra Dímun, Brestir and Beinir realise they are about to be confronted by more than twenty assailants. They urge their sons, who are about twelve and nine years old, to climb the steep cliff path above the rocks to safety. On my first descent of the path, the drop-off and the slippery ground made me feel nauseous. It was here that the young boys had to make their escape from the battle below. They watch as their fathers try to fend off their attackers but eventually, Brestir takes a spear through the stomach from Havgrímur. Knowing he will die, he manages one final blow with his sword, cleaving Havgrímur's shoulder and arm from his body with a fatal strike. Beinir also succeeds in killing at least three of his enemies before eventually falling. And then Tróndur orders that the two young boys be executed. However, Bjarni of Svínoy argues for their lives, and Tróndur is persuaded to spare the boys and take them back to Gøta. Tróndur eventually decides to sell the cousins to a merchant seaman, who allows them to live with his family in Norway for the winter.

Meanwhile, Tróndur seizes the property and farms which had belonged to their fathers. This is a story full of battles, of personal adversity and formidable landscapes, in which heroic men adhere to Viking values and ruthlessness and pragmatism are the keys to survival. The challenges and the stoicism, and a certain lack of sentimentality, chime very much with the attitudes of Faroese society, a culture forged among harsh elements which are unforgiving of dithering or indecision.

The bulk of the Saga follows what happens to the boys, Sigmundur and his cousin Thorir, as they eventually make their way to the court of Earl (Jarl) Haakon, the last pagan king of Norway (937–995). In true archetypal mythic tradition, they impress Haakon with their bravery. Although Sigmundur is two or three years younger than Thorir, he's a better warrior, killing a bear with an axe and leading successful raiding parties into the Baltic Sea and as far south as Anglesey, proving himself to be a cunning tactician in battle. Meanwhile, back in Faroes, Øssur, the son of Havgrímur, has been adopted by Tróndur of Gøta and (when he is old enough) given Brestir's land on Dímun and Skúvoy. Back in Norway, and now respected for his raiding skills and bravery, Sigmundur tells Haakon that he wants to return to Faroes and avenge his father's death. Haakon grants him permission, but first takes him to see a wise woman who gives the king a magical gold arm ring, which he bestows on Sigmundur, warning him to never take it off.

Sigmundur sails back to Faroes, and as a first step, attacks and kills Øssur on the island of Skúvoy. Word is sent to Tróndur of Gøta, and he agrees to meet Sigmundur at the Viking assembly, the *Ting*, in Tórshavn. The two men cannot reach peaceful terms on which to share the rule of the islands, but Sigmundur makes Tróndur agree to travel to Norway and answer to Haakon. Tróndur says he will go to Norway, but then never takes ship. Haakon then decides that Sigmundur and his cousin Thorir will rule over half of Faroes in recompense for the deaths of their fathers and the loss of their lands. Haakon leaves it up to Sigmundur to decide how much property Tróndur should retain in order to make a living. It's fair to say that bad blood remains between Sigmundur and Tróndur.

After a few years, with Sigmundur still fighting for Haakon around the Baltic, there is a change of pace after the king is killed and Olaf Tryggvason becomes overall ruler of Norway, and resolves to make the country and its outposts Christian. He summons Sigmundur to his court and asks him to convert Faroes. Sigmundur duly returns home and summons the *Ting*, where he announces the king's wish that everyone become Christian. Tróndur and a significant number of other men refuse, and Sigmundur is forced to retreat to his farm on Skúvoy for the winter. The next spring, Sigmundur mounts a surprise raid on Tróndur at his farm at Gøta on the island of Eysturoy and forces him to be baptised at knifepoint. Tróndur claims he wants to maintain a peaceful relationship with Sigmundur, but Thorir warns that he is not to be trusted. After another winter on Skúvoy, Sigmundur returns to Norway to tell King Olaf what he has achieved. During his stay the king asks him for the ring that Haakon had given him. When Sigmundur refuses to hand it over, King Olaf accepts that he is honouring Haakon's memory but warns him, 'the ring will bring you bad luck, and will be the death of you.'

In the intervening years, the Saga relates that Sigmundur had children, a daughter named Thora and four sons, Thoralfur, Steingrimur, Brandur and Heri. Tróndur, of course, has not given up opposing Sigmundur, and at the *Ting*, still bitter at his forced conversion, he repeatedly asks for compensation for the death of Øssur, killed by Sigmundur when he raided Skúvoy. Øssur had a son, Leifur, whom Tróndur has taken care of. Sigmundur refuses.

The climax of Sigmundur's story comes one summer day in about 1005, when he has sailed over to Lítla Dímun from Skúvoy, to collect some of his sheep. Thorir, loyal as ever, is with him, along with a man named Einar of Suðuroy. They see ships belonging to Tróndur in the distance and take up a defensive position on the steep-sided cliffs. With his usual tactical cunning, Sigmundur and his friends manage to escape, stealing Tróndur's boat and marooning him with his men on the island. Sigmundur plans to return and kill his enemy once and for all, but Tróndur and his men light a signal fire on Lítla Dímun and are rescued before Sigmundur can return. Shortly afterwards, Tróndur gets a band of around sixty men together and, supported by his splendidly named nephews, Sigurd, Thord the Short and Gaut the Red, sail to Skúvoy and attack Sigmundur's farmhouse. Sigmundur manages to escape with Thorir and Einar through an underground tunnel dug into the hillside. However, Tróndur and his allies chase them to the end of the island, where there is a promontory separated from the main body of Skúvoy by a deep cleft. After some more skirmishing, Sigmundur, Thorir and Einar are forced to jump from the cliffs into the sea. Although Stóra Dímun is closer, the three men are pushed by the current to strike out for Suðuroy, about fifteen kilometres away. As they swim, Einar becomes exhausted, and Sigmundur tows him on his back until Thorir tells him he is carrying a dead man. Soon, and within sight of shore, Thorir says he cannot go on. Sigmundur urges him to keep going and then tries to drag him against the current. Struggling through the waves towards the beach at Sandvík on the north-east coast of Suðuroy, Thorir is finally swept away and drowns.

Sigmundur makes it ashore but collapses from exhaustion and is found the next morning in a pile of seaweed by a local farmer. Unfortunately, the man who finds him is known as 'Thorgrim the Evil', surely a bad omen. He recognises Sigmundur and comments that the great lord has clearly reached a low point. Joined by his sons, Ormstein and Thorstein, Thorgrim decides that they should kill Sigmundur and steal his famous gold arm ring. One early version of the story says that Thorgrim did not have a knife to kill Sigmundur, but instead bent down and tore out his throat with his teeth, and was thereafter nicknamed 'Thor-Dog'. The more sanitised version is that Thorgrim cuts off Sigmundur's head, proving King Olaf's prediction that the golden ring would bring about Sigmundur's doom.

The Saga continues, with Tróndur now in control of all Faroes. He approaches Sigmundur's widow, Thurid, and asks if her daughter Thora will marry Øssur's son Leifur. Thora (Sigmundursdóttir) agrees, on condition that Leifur and Tróndur find out who killed her father. With the help of a little sorcery, in which Tróndur sees a vision of the dead men, he makes Thorgrim the Evil confess to his crime. He is brought before the *Ting* along with his sons, and then all three are hanged. Pleased that her father's murderers have been punished, Sigmundur's daughter marries Øssur's son and lives happily ever after. Sigmundur's farm on Stóra Dímun is left in the hands of his son, Thoralfur.

Interestingly, Sigmundur has all the attributes of a classical hero. But, he is not necessarily regarded as the 'goody' in modern Faroes. Equally, the seemingly dastardly Tróndur of Gøta is admired as a fiercely independent man, resisting attempts to have a foreign religion imposed upon his homeland, and reluctant to submit to edicts issued by a foreign kingdom. Both men have their positive attributes, and the saga clearly doesn't end with any suggestion that Tróndur has escaped his comeuppance. This kind of duality, this willingness to accommodate different views are themes that resonate even now with the islanders, especially when they consider their ongoing relationship with Denmark, their refusal to join the European Union and their increasing pride in very unique aspects of Faroese culture.

Climbing the cliff path from Rakhella up towards the

farmstead on Stóra Dímun is frightening for anyone not used to it, and needs significant care even if you are. Aside from the almost permanently damp foot-wide track and the sheer drop to one side, there is the constant threat of falling rocks from above. Clinging to the rusty hawser that acts as a handrail for part of the descent, I imagine myself being a nine-year-old boy trying to climb the cliff face while my father, outnumbered by his enemies, fights for his life on the shore below. Having witnessed his death, the idea of being taken to live with his killer and then sent into exile aboard a Viking trading ship is barely imaginable to us today. But, knowing the legend, which contains so many verifiable incidents and recognisable landmarks, makes being in this raw landscape a powerful experience.

The challenges of life on Dímun weren't confined to the Viking era. In 1874, a parish priest came to give one of his bi-annual sermons on the island and after conducting the service in the tiny church, he slipped to his death from the path at Kleivin. It's said he had turned to check that this wife was all right, and was offering her his hand when he lost his balance.

Clergymen were not the only species to end their days on Dímun. In his comprehensive study of Faroes bird-life, the British naturalist Colonel Henry Feilden related that the island was the last place in the country where a great auk (*Pinguinus impennis*) was seen alive. Like the dodo, the bird was cursed with an incompatible combination of flightlessness, a lack of timidity and tastiness. Once common in Faroes, and Iceland, Greenland and Newfoundland, it became totally extinct sometime in the 1850s, with the last nesting pair destroyed on Eldey Island in Iceland in 1844.

Known variously as the 'Magellanic goose', 'woggin', 'king murre' and 'garefowl', the auk was the original 'penguin', a name derived either from Celtic – *pen gwyn* or Breton *pen gouin* – both meaning 'white head'. In summer plumage, the auks developed a white flash in front of the eye, though the rest of the head was actually black. Etymologists argue whether the term may have instead referred to the guano-covered rocks on which auks were found. Or, perhaps, it came from the Latin for 'fat'– *pinguis*. In any case, the common name 'penguin' was applied to its southern flightless cousins only later, and because of their similarity to the 'northern penguin'. Defenceless and, according to the American naturalist James Orton, 'known only to utter a gurgling sound' it looked very much like a razorbill (*Alca torda*), but was about four times bigger, at almost three feet tall.

The Danish naturalist and collector Ole Worm (1588 – 1654) famously kept a pet great auk in Copenhagen, among the collection catalogued as his *History of Very Rare Things, Natural and Artificial, Domestic and Exotic*. The auk in Worm's Museum was known to have come from 'the Færoes, on the shores of which it is abundant'. His copper-plate etching of the bird, published in 1655, was the first illustration of an auk drawn from a living specimen. The first modern illustration of the bird was made by the naturalist Clusius (Charles de L'Éscluse) at the University of Leiden. It appeared in his *Exoticorum libri decem* (Ten Books on Exotic Life Forms) of 1605, and based on dead specimens again sent from Faroes. The poor woggins were also periodically kept alive for a few months in Louis XVI's menagerie at Versailles.

When Feilden visited Faroes in 1872, he recorded a visit to Skúvoy 'in the company of Herr Sysselmand Winther, who took me to the cottage of an old man, Jan Hansen, now 81 years of age. He is believed to be the last man alive in the islands who remembers seeing a gare-fowl in Faeroe, and from a comparison of dates it would appear to be the last recorded instance of the appearance of the bird in these islands. The old man, who is now blind, told me that on 1st July 1808 he went with a crew to the Great Dimon for the purpose of catching rock birds: upon a ledge at the base of the cliffs of that island they came across a single garfuglir, which was captured; this bird weighed 9 Danish pounds (4,5kg or 10 English pounds) and on the division of the birds at the conclusion of the fowling, was deemed equivalent to six guillemots.' Feilden also noted that 'from the attention the natives pay to the arrival and departure of sea-birds, with their frequent visits to the Fuglebergs, and constant journeyings in boats around the islands, it would be very unlikely for any gare-fowl to have since escaped observation.' Colonel Feilden also interviewed some men from Vaagoe (Vágar) who had been birding towards Iceland in 1813. The Faroese men were able to catch more than a dozen gare-fowl along with 200 guillemots and numerous gannets, collecting them from rocks which the Icelanders were not brave enough to climb. He notes solemnly, 'The men did not leave a single dead gare-fowl behind them but the boat was so full of birds they had to leave many dead guillemots on the ledge'. The last great auk ever seen in the UK was captured off Stac an Armin, St Kilda, in 1840. Three fishermen tied its legs together and kept it captive on board their boat, until after three days a storm blew up. Fearing for their lives, they decided that the auk was in reality 'a maelstrom causing witch' and beat it to death with a stick. On 3rd June, 1844, Jón Brandsson and Sigurður Ísleifsson are recorded as finding a nesting pair of great auks on the island of Eldey at the south-western tip of Iceland. Knowing their value as museum specimens, the fishermen strangled the adult birds, and, perhaps accidently, their companion Ketill Ketilsson stood on the last egg and crushed it. There is also an unconfirmed, but highly probable sighting of a single great auk swimming off Newfoundland in 1853. Feilden was told that a Sandoy man had a great auk beak in his possession when he died in 1845, but that years later it seemed to have disappeared, and no one could say what had happened to it.

Even without contributions from great auks, the seabird guano on Stóra Dímun is part of the reason why the island continues to produce healthy sheep and vegetables. Like generations before them, Eva and Jógvan Jón continue to plant their crops of potato, turnips and kohlrabi on the flat land between the farmhouse and the lighthouse. The white turnips are small and sweet, and if you peel off the outer skin you can eat them raw, like apples. In autumn, Eva and Jógvan Jón are joined by friends and extended family in the frenetic period when the sheep must be gathered from the high ground and rams brought up the perilous path from the Grønaskor, where they have been fattened on grass fertilised by tens of thousands of seabirds. Much of the island is known as *feitilendi*, the highest quality of 'fattening land'.

The helicopter comes now, and the children on the farm can have violin lessons via Skype. It is no longer the 'loneliest farmhouse in the world'. But some of the immemorial past remains fixed here. And it is comforting. Twice a day the cow in the byre next to the kitchen is milked in the traditional way by one of the family sitting on a simple, two-legged wooden stool. Eva coaxes the gentle-natured cow tenderly, with a skill honed over a lifetime on the farm. The warm creamy milk comes in powerful streams that make the bucket sing. Around Eva, the steam from the cow's flank rises in the dimly lit shed, suffusing the weak light from the electric bulb. The animal stalls are worn and weathered by thousands of hooves and teeth and rumps and horns rubbing against them over hundreds of years. Strong earthy animal smells mix with the tang of fermenting hay, and the richly burnished wood is cast into a timeless chiaroscuro image.

Ravens III

May

The three raven chicks have their feathers now, though they are not very active when the parents are away from the nest. After checking that they are all alive and well, I use my time to observe everything that goes on around the gorge. Tell-tale signs on the grass show that something has been using the cliff as a feeding spot. I have taken to treasure hunting, finding the bones of other birds, and more than once the bleached skull of an oystercatcher. I admire the marble-sized dome and

the long distinctive beak the colour of carotene. I can't be sure that the remains have been left by the ravens. There are great skuas here, nesting up on the higher ground, and I have seen them cruising above the gull colony further up the coast. Often, I find the thorax of a bigger bird, a bloodied bone box picked clean and emptied of its internal organs. Sometimes the ribcage is still attached to the wings, or there will be a pair of legs nearby, bones stripped even of gristle, but with the flaccid flaps of wrinkled skin on their wide webbed feet untouched.

All along the highest parts of the ravine there are outcrops of rose root, stumpy-leaved and topped with the first showing of distinctive flat golden flowers. They stand upright, leaning out over the water in thick clumps clinging to crevices in the rock wall and colonising the grassy lip of the cleft. The Vikings used the plants as a calming medicine.

On the highest and smallest ledges there are nesting fulmars, perhaps twenty or more on the cliffside where the ravens live. They produce a constant throaty grumbling, interrupted by occasional higher-pitched rapid *gak-gak-gak* cries when anyone invades their small piece of territory. The noise rises to a pitch when I come near to the gorge, but settles again as soon as I take my place on the bank and hunker down in my viewing spot. They have not laid their eggs yet, but they are securing their perches on any tiny patch of grass with enough space to lay their single egg, and preen.

I too sit in a little sheltered hollow, hugging the ground to evade the wind. There is a grassy bowl about a metre from the edge of the gorge, perhaps an old sheep scrape that has become overgrown. I am about five metres higher than the ravens' nest and only need to raise my head above the lip of the bowl to see them. I stay low most of the time in case the adults return with food. Mostly, the chicks lie like sleeping puppies with their chins resting on the edge of the nest, edgeless forms wedged so tightly together that I can't see where one raven ends and the other begins.

I am never bored here. Beside me, the grass reveals an endless range of shades. Last year's dead growth is still visible, a thatch of old gold hiding the strong green fresh shoots below. Clumps of moss sprout everywhere, bulbous colonies as varied in colour as a forest in autumn. Patches vary from bright lime to deep red, rust brown and traces of pink on the fresh tips. The tiny crevices on the cliffs are also beginning to show new growth, and flowering plants are producing spots of colour, safely out of reach of the wandering sheep. I can find marsh violets an inch high, pale pink and lace white with stamens as fine as fishing line and tiny petals striated by blood-dark veins. All but lost in the new growth of grass are dog violets, leaves the vivid purple of a Catholic funeral robe.

4

The Long Swim

Skúvoy is another place of legend. Tummas Frank Joensen knows all of the stories, and every comment and observation triggers another anecdote about the island and the people who live there. He and his wife Elisabeth make me welcome in their tidy little house in the centre of Skúvoy village. It's neatly clad in wood and painted watery green as the shallows of a Faroese rockpool. Like all of the houses in Skúvoy village, it bears a name plaque rather than a number, a wooden board saying *Norði á Fløtti*. Tummas says it means 'to the north of the flat field'.

He and Elisabeth are both life-long supporters of Liverpool FC, and with a big match coming up, they had hopes that an English guest on the island would be keen to talk about their team's prospects and watch the game. At breakfast in their cosy kitchen, the radio is on in the background and the news is all about football. Most people here follow an English league team, and there's a particularly strong affection for Liverpool. The radio broadcast is, of course, in Faroese, so I'm not following the fine detail when Elisabeth gets up from the table to turn the volume up loud. In honour of Liverpool FC, they are playing

'You'll Never Walk Alone' and she sings along, tunefully and unselfconsciously. Perhaps because I'm there, and perhaps because I am not joining in, Tummas sits quietly drumming his fingers in time to the tune while I eat my toast. He watches the weather from the large kitchen window, judging whether we should set out for the far end of the island. When the music finishes, Elisabeth asks me if I know the song, and she and Tummas seem reassured when I acknowledge somewhat evasively that it is very popular in England. Elisabeth isn't confident speaking English, although she follows everything I say. Tummas is a great talker, and passionate about Skúvoy and how much he wishes more people would visit.

A pot of tea appears, and their son Jón, a tall lean man in his early thirties with the fresh complexion and rosy cheeks of someone who's always outdoors, joins us. He asks if I follow football, and once again I have to confess my lack of in-depth knowledge. He and his father exchange a subtle glance that tells me clearly I have disappointed everyone. Jón is the youngest person on Skúvoy, and has only recently returned from another island to work on some municipal projects – including digging a new mains sewerage system for the village. Now is the time when the rams will be turned out into the infields for summer grazing, and he will help out with that too. He and Tummas explain that the island population is declining, and that there are now only twenty-three permanent residents, with an average age of sixty-five. The village school closed over a decade ago, but Tummas, who's almost seventy, remembers when there were 140 people in the village, eighteen kids in the school and a few extra who would come in the spring and stay all summer to help out with farming. The sheep are still here, with around a thousand ewes on Skúvoy, divided into five herds. In autumn the owners and helpers will come from other islands to do their share of gathering and slaughtering.

Fifty metres above the sea, and almost exactly in the middle of the east coast of the island, the thirty houses that make up the settlement cluster tight together, beside the Árdalsá river, which is fed by the slopes of a shallow-sided valley that sweep down from Skúvoy's highest point, Knútur. Sheep graze the banks of the river, wagtails and rock pipits flitter above mossy dry-stone walls, and there's a church spire poking up above the seascape beyond. It's very much how a valley in the west of Ireland might have looked fifty years ago. The houses have typically small Faroese gardens, many of them boasting patches of scruffy-looking rhubarb, and I have seen some gooseberry and redcurrant bushes, which somehow survive the wind. There are no cars here, but there is an old Massey Ferguson 135 tractor (not manufactured since 1975) outside the last house on the north edge of the village. It was once shiny red, but the salty air has faded it to an old-sock shade of pink. It's still in use though the barely yellow hubcaps are speckled with rust, textured and freckled as prettily as a bird's egg. Northwards, a narrow coastal track meanders past strips of pasture separated by sheepwire fences. Skúvoy slopes east-low to west-high, and the cliffs are mighty.

At the end of the coastal track, which is tarred for about

a kilometre, a sheep gate opens onto a wide sweeping plain where dozens of skuas nest. There are fast soaring, streamlined Arctic skuas with pointed double tail feathers extending behind them like the flights on a dart. Their cousins are here too, the bigger barrel-chested great skuas in their rich chocolate-brown plumage. After visiting Faroes, the Danish nineteenth-century naturalist Jørgen Landt observed that skuas 'form the transition from the gulls to the bird of prey, resembling the one in body, plumage, and food, and the other in bill, claws, flight and predatory propensities and are the object of aversion to every other bird.' Landt's observations were meticulous and he is one of the few outsiders to record the unique way in which the Faroese measured time. They divided the day into what he called *ökter* – eight three-hour portions named after points of the compass. Twelve midnight was called 'north' while twelve noon was referred to as 'south'. Six am became simply 'east' and six pm was 'west'. Ninety-minute intervals were 'half-eighths', so that ten thirty pm would be north-north-west.

Skúvoy means 'island of skuas', and they have lived here longer than men. They were once eaten – several thousand a year on Skúvoy, captured as fledglings and pinioned, so they could be fattened up before slaughter. Skua is the only Faroese word in the English language, a simplified version of *skúgvur* (pronounced *skik-vur*). The word, like much else here, feels ancient, and across the narrow sound, on the much larger island of Sandoy, some of the earliest evidence of human settlement in Faroes has been found. It shows that whoever lived here in the fourth century grew barley and burned peat for fuel. That's surely another Irish link, or seems like it to me.

Later, when the Faroese Saga was written (in about AD 1200), it was Skúvoy where the Christian hero, Sigmundur Brestisson, had his farm, and it was from the cliffs at the northern end of the island where he and his companions leaped into the sea to swim all the way to Suðuroy fifteen kilometres away. Before Sigmundur's adventures, the Saga holds that the first man to settle Faroes was Grímur Kamban, who fled to the islands to escape the rule of the Norwegian king, Harald Fairhair, who reigned from AD 872 to 930. Viking scholars say Kamban's name has Celtic origins and means 'crooked or lame one', and that he may have come from Ireland, the Hebrides or even the Isle of Man. If he wasn't the first man to live in Faroes, then he may have been the first to permanently settle after the earlier Celtic monks were driven away, or simply died out. I am reminded of the monks who staved off Viking incursions near to where I lived in Ireland, and around Strangford Lough especially, not far from where I was born. On a tiny island with a prominent knoll, there are the remains of a small monastic settlement and a defensive round tower with views across the water. It dates from around the same time that Faroes was settled, and it was a place where I loved to sit and watch the sunset, particularly in winter when the shapes of the surrounding islands made it seem like a landscape out of time.

Tummas is keen for me to see Sigmundur's cliffs at the northern tip of Skúvoy, where he was sent onto the narrow ledges as a boy to collect guillemot eggs. We set out together on a bright spring morning, following the farm track as it climbs towards the outfield. Skúvoy village sits at the top of the short steep concrete slipway from the harbour, sheltered from the worst of the west winds by a long high mountain ridge behind it. The ferry from Sandoy trundles back and forth on a thirty-five-minute journey (as often as not by request), sometimes up to five times a day in summer. The sky is clear, but it's windy and if it strengthens later, the afternoon ferry may not run. There's also a helicopter service four days each week, which cuts out the need for a second ferry journey from Sandoy to Gamlarætt for anyone who needs to get to Tórshavn. Tummas watches the fjord constantly. He tells me he spent thirty-seven years as a merchant seaman on the ferries and confesses that he misses the sea and that it was the best time of his life. He explains the danger of the changeable winds in Faroes, and how when tide and wind combine unfavourably the conditions can quickly become deadly. Tides are always described in Faroes as *vestfall* or *eystfall* – westerly or easterly – and Tummas warns about what happens when the wind shifts westerly and meets an easterly tide. The opposing forces create a long rolling wave, and he says that not understanding that combination can be the difference between life and death here.

In his sitting room, Tummas has a reminder of the perils of sailing on the high seas in northern latitudes. In the corner, close to the dining table, is a professionally made model boat in a glass case. It's a combined passenger and cargo ship, the M/S *Hans Hedtoft*, sometimes called the 'modern *Titanic*'. Tummas tells me that his uncle, Hans

Richard Jacobsen, was thirty-one years old and second mate when the brand new ship set sail from Copenhagen for Greenland in January 1959. The 2800-tonne vessel set a new speed record for the outward journey, and left Julianehåb to return to Denmark on 29th January. The following day, the ship sent an SOS saying it had struck an iceberg twenty miles south of Greenland's Cape Farewell. Even though it was constructed with seven watertight compartments, the *Hedtoft* was taking in water and the engine room was flooding. Almost four hours after the first SOS was sent, a final transmission was received and then nothing more. Forty crew and fifty-five passengers – including six small children – died, and no trace of the ship was ever found other than a life-buoy which was washed up on a Greenlandic beach nine months later. The *Hans Hedtoft* is the only recorded sinking by an iceberg with loss of life since the *Titanic*. Tummas is emotional when he recounts the story, even though he was only a boy when his uncle drowned.

Tummas has many stories about the dangers of the local weather. One Skúvoy legend holds that in the eighteenth century eight young girls from the village set out one afternoon to collect milk from the cows in the hills when a thick mist came down. All but one of the milkmaids decided to hold hands and walk together back along the coast to safety. Unable to see the edge of the cliffs, they fell to their deaths, pulling one another into the sea. Only the girl who had refused to hold hands survived.

We pass through the sheep gate and onto the open ground heading north. There are great skuas in the skies and dotted about on the grass. It's the start of nesting time. Several birds have colonised little hillocks in the grass from where they watch out over their territory. Tummas brandishes a walking stick, which he says he will use to ward them off if they dive-bomb us. Many of the birds have spent the winter in the Bay of Biscay, close to the Spanish coast. or in North African waters, but they are back here to breed. We follow a line across a vast open moor with views to Sandoy in the east. Across the water, sheer and dizzying, are the high cliffs at Lonin where I have watched men descend hundreds of metres in search of plump fresh fulmar eggs. After almost an hour, we reach a ridge where the land dips steeply, Fagridalur, a sweeping plain of green cut through by a small stream leading due north. In the distance, there is a promontory, which Tummas calls Høvdin. It's separated from the valley by a deep steep-sided gully, and despite his age and his walking stick, he heads for it at surprising speed.

Halfway across the open ground, I hear the swift rush of air as a great skua sweeps in past my head. It doesn't call out, but simply dives at us, and Tummas raises his stick perpendicular to his head, like a roofless umbrella. He casts around, walking towards a patch of ground where he begins to creep carefully in circles. 'Here', he says, pointing with his free hand. There are two large eggs on the grass in a bowl where the adult's body has hunkered down. The grass is brown and flattened, hay-like, but not woven together into a structure like a proper nest. Perfectly camouflaged, and very hard to spot, the eggs are dull coppery green flecked with peat brown. They have the sheen of an old coin burnished by being passed through thousands of pairs of hands. The parent birds are both circling close by, and alarmed, uttering a sharp growling bark, unmistakeably angry. We move away quickly, not wanting to frighten them off the nest for too long.

Tummas is back to his story-telling as we continue alongside the stream. He says that this valley, isolated and unvisited most of the time, is known as the place where a girl named Rannvá lived in exile several hundred years ago. Some stone ruins in the valley are supposedly the remains of her house. One version of the story is that Rannvá was sent from Skúvoy to Tórshavn for the national holiday Ólavsøka, the day when the parliament, or *Ting*, was convened. During her visit, she attracted attention from a man who arranged to meet her the following year. On their second meeting, she became pregnant. At the time, in the sixteenth century, it was a capital crime in Faroes to have a child out of wedlock. However, when she refused to name the father of the child, instead of being hanged – or publicly drowned in the harbour – she was exiled to this valley and forbidden to go into the village. Another version of the story, a Faroese version of Cinderella, says she was exiled to the valley by a wicked stepmother who wanted her father's farm, although there was no handsome prince to come to her rescue. However, Rannvá had the last laugh, as the Black Death came to Skúvoy, killing everyone on the island except for her and her son.

We reach the ravine that divides the open sweep of Fagridalur from the domed headland at the northern tip of Skúvoy. Not far from the edge, a large rock stands proud of the grass and all alone. It's known as the *Tróndarsteinur* (Tróndur's Stone), and is close to the spot where Sigmundur Brestisson jumped across the ravine to escape pursuit. Tróndur is supposed to have lain down beside the stone and conjured some kind of spell to help him defeat Sigmundur. The stone, covered in lichen, looks as if it's been sprayed with gold paint that is now peeling in the wind and rain. It has the rich depth of egg yolk against the basalt, the most vibrant natural colour on the island. Tummas is proud that Sigmundur came from Skúvoy, and says that another day he will take me to see his grave.

Tummas leads the way along the precipitous grass track to the ravine, where we rest on an old stone ruin, the remains of a winter sheep shelter, close to the water. Elisabeth has made us a picnic lunch – fermented lamb with dark bread she has baked herself. We make no mess, but around us the ground is littered with empty limpet shells, left by the birds. Tummas admits that although he walks the island regularly, he hasn't been down to the bottom of the ravine for years. He wants to explore the foreshore, so we clamber onto the boulder-strewn ledge that is the closest thing to a beach on Skúvoy. The rocks are large, bowling ball-sized, and tumbled together in just one accessible area close to the north-easternmost point of the island. A sheep, eating seaweed at the high-water mark, ignores us. Tummas says that some people claim they can taste it in the meat when a sheep has eaten a lot of seaweed. We pick our way out to the headland, beachcombing and watching a large group of eider ducks surfing in the violent swell that sweeps around the point. 'The rougher the better,' Tummas says. 'They enjoy big waves.'

Tummas has found a sea monster. He calls me over to inspect the grisly remains wedged in between the boulders. It's rigid like very old leather, a withered clump of meat-red skin, but in places where there is fur it has been bleached by sun and salt. There is a small skull, or at least the top of a skull, but no jaw or teeth attached. Fine sand, seashells and seaweed have mingled with the remains, which are twisted and tangled like a sodden piece of clothing straight out of a washing machine. There is a smell too, something sweetly cloying. I can identify part of a backbone, and a tangle of thick blackened tubes attached to what remains of the upper spine, which could be blood vessels or intestines. And there is one small elongated flipper, with what seem like finger bones visible through the dried flesh. The digits are splayed wide, and there are inch-long sharp claws protruding from the yellowing hide, which is as taught and faded as an old drumskin. It is a baby seal. There are other bones scattered among the rocks nearby. I pick up a small scapula, dry and cleaned of any meat by the birds. It fits neatly into my palm, light as a plastic bottle-top. The semicircular outside edge has a beautiful curve, finely rounded like a leaf. I slip it into my pocket as Tummas points with his stick to the steep cone of land above us. 'Will you go up there?' he asks, pointing up at the headland cliffs. It's very steep, and I have confessed my wariness of high slippery ground, but Tummas seems determined to spend as much time here as he can.

We climb steadily, breathlessly, towards a point on the tip of Skúvoy high above the sea. It means crabbing up the grass and holding onto the ground in places until we reach a small flattened promontory proud of the sheer northern cliffs. Tummas says this is close to Krákuspíld, the spot where Sigmundur would have jumped into the sea. We are very near the edge of the cliff face, and the Atlantic is a swirling shark-grey mass more than a hundred metres below. I can see Suðuroy in the distance, although the damp air makes the island look as if it's behind frosted glass. The idea of jumping into the water is terrifying enough, and surviving several hours in the frigid sea unimaginable.

Tummas and I are able to perch on the cliff edge and watch the birds roosting. 'I was seven when I came here and went out for birds' eggs the first time,' he explains. 'In those days there were so many birds. In 1974, I remember, we collected about 5000 guillemot eggs.'

It's hard to imagine how rich the birdlife of Faroes was a century ago. One Danish ornithologist estimated that before the Second World War, as many as 80,000 guillemot eggs could be taken in a week on Skúvoy. Men were roped together, and stayed out on the cliff ledges overnight, one on watch to make sure no one rolled over and fell in their sleep. As well as the eggs, fledgling chicks were captured after they jumped from the cliff face and spent their first weeks as swimmers still fed by their parents. Adults were taken too, sometimes caught by men in boats at sea. One technique was to nail a stuffed guillemot upright on a wooden plank with dozens of snares made from horsehair attached to it. The plank would then be tethered to a buoy. Other birds, lured by the decoy, would land on the plank and be trapped. It's easy to see why their penguin-like gait would quickly get them entangled. There are guillemots all along the ledges ahead of us, with nine or ten huddled close on a small scoop in the rock-face. These are common guillemots, elegant birds with small delicate skulls and fine pointed beaks. Their breasts and tummies are pure white, and everything else is a delicate shade of brown, as if they have lain on their front in a tub of cocoa powder. They face inwards, with their backs to the sea, a sign, according to Tummas, that they have eggs. Those eggs are often rich deep shades of verdigris and spattered with coarse marks that look as if they have been made by a deranged hand wielding a quill pen.

On the ledge, the guillemots shuffle awkwardly about on their tarsi, the long bone connecting the 'ankle' to the feet. Of the nine birds closest to me, three are of the bridled variant, with a thin white line encircling the eye and extending down the side of the head. They look as if they are wearing wire-framed glasses. All of the birds are the same species, the 'spectacles' are just a simple plumage variation that increases in frequency the further north the birds live. Guillemots in England are rarely bridled, but up here and in Iceland and Norway, as many as half of the birds in a colony may show the variation. Some ornithologists speculate that the white eye stripe may somehow help the birds when diving for fish in dimly lit seas, perhaps confusing their prey. The only fact about the two colour variations that has been proven is that the chicks of mixed pairs seem to grow slightly faster than those born to parents of the same variation. In Victorian times, the birds with the eye stripe were classified for a time as 'crying guillemots'. I can hear their warbling as they cluster together, a gentle persistent wave of high-pitched chatter like the drifting noise of shrieking from a school playground.

* * *

I return to Fagridalur on other days, alone. The great skuas watch me balefully as I pass through their territory. The massive natural bowl of the valley is mesmerisingly peaceful, never silent, but free of all unnatural sounds. The individual cries of the birds are easily discernible, and the wind soughs in my ears without anger. I am happy to sit on the lip of the ravine watching the birds coming in from the open sea, and listen to the rhythmic pounding of the ocean against the base of the headland. In this spot, close to Krákuspíld, where Sigmundur made his desperate leap, it is the kittiwakes and the fulmars that seem to dominate the ledges. The small stream that cuts across the middle of the valley is pure and clean, bordered by bright green moss. It falls over the edge of the island and down the rockface without becoming a violent torrent. Kittiwakes come in ones and twos and pin themselves, bat-like, to carbuncular footholds in the rocks beside the water. They often seek out river or rainwater during the breeding season, although like most gulls, they can drink seawater, excreting the salt from a special nasal gland. But now, open-beaked, they extend their necks and let the sweet water seep into their mouths. I wonder if they feel more secure this way, less vulnerable to skuas, which might swoop from above if they drank from the stream banks on the open ground.

In the grass, close to where a skua pair is nesting, I find fish bones. There are scaly indigestible pectoral fins, lacy surfaces ribbed and veined, trapping the light in their pores like fragments of shattered safety glass. I pick up half a dozen tiny vertebrae, clean and white. Almost weightless, they look like miniature draughts pieces, and the faintest breath of wind makes them tumble and skitter across my hand. As I climb the steep side of Fagridalur, I can see clearly across the water to Sandoy in the east. Cresting the ridge, there is just the open moorland sloping down in a gentle gradient towards the village. It is cool, but the sun is shining and the fjord is free of white caps today. It glimmers, a thousand shades of antique sapphire.

In the late afternoon, I walk back towards the village, counting the skua pairs. On this part of the island, the smaller Arctic birds are outnumbered ten to one. It is the large brown bonxies that heckle me as I pass across the high moor and approach the sheep gate. In a dip in the land, which turns out to be a trickling beck no more than a footprint wide, I see the upraised speckled wings of a great skua. It is clearly attacking something, stabbing furiously at the ground. I walk closer, expecting to see it fly away from some kind of smaller prey. But it's so intent on plucking at its victim that I can walk right up to it, unnoticed. Then I see that it has another skua on its back and half submerged in the beck, which is just an inch or two deep. There is enough water to make its feathers slick and dark, and the victim seems half drowned, motionless and barely fighting back. I gently nudge the aggressor with my boot, and still it stabs and worries the other bird like a terrier with a rat. I put the toe of my boot between the birds, and finally the attacker lets go and hops away. The other skua looks dead. Its head is on the edge of the beck, and one wing and most of the body are trailing in the water. Its eyes are open, and there is a barely perceptible shudder as I bend down to see what wounds it may have. Cautiously, at arm's length, I lift it from the water and lay it on the grass, virtually moribund. I retreat a little way, and then, after half a minute, it flaps its wings, righting itself and shaking its feathers as if it has just been bathing. I am convinced it must have mortal injuries. But then, after a few seconds more, it stretches its wings, stands and walks a few steps and takes off, flying away fast and leaving one small tail feather drifting to the ground. I rinse my hands in the beck, which is nerve-jinglingly chilled even though the sun feels warm on my back. Everywhere, patches of *mýrisólja*, bright yellow marsh marigolds, are appearing on the banks of the streams. Island wisdom says they bloom when the guillemots lay. As I walk back into the village, the air is filled with starlings. They are carrying scraps of moss in their beaks and diving into the stone walls around the infield. There is abundance in the air.

I smell dinner as I walk in, and discover that Elisabeth has been roasting *skrápur* – Manx shearwaters. I have not seen them often, just once in any number when I spotted thousands bobbing on a glassy sea off Pembrokeshire late one summer's evening. Small blackened birds stuffed with onion emerge from the main oven, and she brings freshly boiled potatoes and carrots to the table. Her son Jón joins us for dinner, soon tucking in and tearing apart a bird with his fingers in the traditional way, oblivious to the grease dripping down his fingers and palms. He is bemused that I have never eaten shearwater before, and tells me that they only catch a few during fledgling season, in August. The meat is rich and juicy, and perfect with the potatoes. I eat two whole birds, while Jón manages three.

After dinner, Jón says he will take Tummas's rams out of the shed where they have spent the winter. These are the *veðrur*, rams born last year and kept for fattening up rather than breeding. The sheep shed is only a few metres away from the house, an ancient stone building with a weathered wooden door. The inside is dim, and there is the strong smell of urine-soaked hay and the steaming warmth of the animals. Five rams jostle together in a raised wooden pen. Tummas talks to them and they peer inquisitively from the stall, sticking their heads over the wooden beams to see if he has food. It's common to keep rams inside for their first winter, after the tupping season, so that the lambing is controlled and predictable. But they'll go out now to fatten up over summer. They skitter on the wooden boards as Jón starts getting ready to drag them from the stall. Outside, Tummas and Elisabeth busy themselves with hitching a trailer to their ATV. There is a plank for the rams to walk up into the trailer but they must be brought out one by one, and there is no way to herd them from the shed except on foot, grasping them by the horns. There are four white rams and one that is all black except for a white star on his nose, and he's clearly the boss. Jón takes the first animal out and tells me to bring a second, one of the white rams. He's reluctant to leave the pen, and I need a hand on each horn to drag him from the gloomy shed, shuffling along with his body between my knees so he won't buck and twist away from me. The horns feel mildly greasy, lubricated with lanolin from rubbing up against the other males. He jumps as I lead him out of the cosy sheep shed, and manhandling him up the gangway is a workout. We repeat the process until we have all five rams inside the trailer; I climb up behind Jón on the motorcycle-style seat and we head off towards the infield.

Tummas owns land at the upper end of the valley that stretches away west from the village. When we get there,

Jón manoeuvres the ATV and its cargo through a gap in the wire fence and drives some distance into the field. Tummas is not far behind on a second ATV, and Elisabeth has a plastic tub filled with food for the rams. The fence is tied shut with orange nylon twine and then, one by one, as the sheep are coaxed out of the trailer, they dash away from the vehicle. Elisabeth rattles the feed and lets out a trilling call, but food is not on their minds and they sprint up the field. No sooner are they all out and together than they start sparring. Each ram seems programmed to look for a rival, and they immediately nudge one another and then take a step or two backwards to butt heads. I notice that none challenges the black ram. To me, the four white rams are indistinguishable, but two of them begin to fight seriously. They make short pronking charges, lifting both front feet off the ground and clashing heads mid-air. *Crack!* Like a gunshot. Time and again they clash, and both males soon have blood seeping from their skulls at the base of their horns. 'They will sometimes kill each other,' observes Tummas. '*Yew-ee, yew-ee!*' Elisabeth calls, shaking her bucket, but the novelty of being in the open air and the prospect of a fight is too distracting. After ten minutes of repeated clashes, they seem exhausted and trot off to join the dominant ram on a hummock, from where he can survey the entire large field.

This week Jón has agreed to transport several groups of rams into the fields for other, absent farmers. These males are all handsome animals, startling for their vigour and strength. Everything about them is designed for procreation, and they exude maleness with strong elegant horns above a curiously bulbous snout. Their aggression is never directed at us when we handle them, although Jón warns against petting them when they are in the trailer in case they trap my fingers against the metal sides. 'You will have a broken hand,' he observes matter-of-factly. He tolerates my willingness to help, but I sense he thinks I'm not tough enough to do much serious work.

Each morning in the days and weeks that follow, Elisabeth or Tummas will walk up the farm track from the village with a tub of sheep biscuits. They enter the field and rattle it to entice the rams closer, keeping them used to human contact. Tummas tells me it will tame them a little and help make rounding them up easier in the autumn.

One evening, after a dinner of *rognaknettir* – dumplings made with raisins, cod roe and the fat from around a sheep's rectum – Tummas offers to take me to see the island church. There is no one else about as we cross the little wooden bridge over the river. The church is a typical Faroese design with wooden pews and a hand-knitted altar cloth made by local women. He and Elisabeth are regular churchgoers and he is proud of this well-kept building. Outside, a narrow strip of flat leads along the coast towards the southern tip of the island, and about 500 metres from the river is the village cemetery. There are skeins of sea mist hanging over the sound between Skúvoy and Sandoy, wispy as contrails. Tummas solemnly shows me the graves of his relatives, before leading me to an irregular headstone in a corner of the graveyard. This is the *Sigmundarsteinur* marking the spot where Sigmundur

Brestisson, Faroes' first Christian convert, was buried in 1005. There is something typically Faroese about this modest monument, which is barely knee high. A more natural-looking gravestone cannot be imagined. Rough hewn and unpolished, it seems like a geological eruption from the ground. There's a neatly incised cross extending to the edges of the rock, which is encrusted with cement-coloured lichen.

One evening, Tummas offers to show me the high western edge of the island. There is no wind as we ride the ATV up the track past the rams and over the Árdalsá river. The ground becomes boggy and Tummas picks his way between muddy sinkholes and boulders, feeling his way up towards the high ground. The bike lurches, pressing me against his shoulders as he negotiates the rough pasture. At the cliffs we dismount and walk the last few hundred metres to a viewpoint from where we can see the birds wheeling above Hæddin and Snati. The fulmars rule here, impervious to the buffeting updrafts on the 300-metre cliffs. We move north a little to reach the highest point on the west coast, a small nipple of a promontory at Knútur. I climb the last few metres to the trig point, 391.76 metres above the sea. The northern end of Suðuroy is visible across the water, another island floating as if in a dream. The sun is almost on the horizon, and the light is soft. I'm the king of the castle. Below me, Tummas is sitting at the very cliff edge, as if he is on the bridge of his boat. He is utterly at ease, gazing out over a polished sea.

Ravens IV

Late May

Today is wet, with a heavy mist at the mouth of the fjord making Streymoy barely visible. I can only see the base of the opposite near shore. It has become a ghostland where sea and mountains merge behind a fuzzy curtain. The high hillsides beside me are cloaked in a blanket of moisture that deadens all sound except the squelch of my boots as I walk past the sheep pen and into the outfield. There is death here too. In a shallow puddle beside the farm track, I find a freshly killed oystercatcher. It lies on its back, wings spread open like a grotesque snow angel to reveal a bloody meatless breast. Sodden feathers trail in the water and one bright orange-rimmed eye shines back from the surface of the puddle. That long questing beak is buried in the moss. It looks like a skua kill, but the ravens or the gulls will soon take the rest.

Approaching the gorge from the seaward end, I surprise the adult ravens. They were not on the nest itself, but sheltering in a sea cave at the very base of the cliffs, just a few metres above the high-tide mark. The cave is invisible from the grassy slope where I have taken to hiding, and I only found it by crawling to the edge and leaning out. I wonder now if they may have been inside sometimes when I have been on the mound watching the nest. Peering over the edge is enough of an intrusion to draw the birds from their hiding place with a rough *krork krorking* cry, and they fly past no more than five metres away from my eye level. The muscular beat of their wings is amplified by the narrow walls of the cleft. One heads seawards and the other peels off inland, cresting the rounded hummock of the high ground on the southern edge of the cliffs. I suspect they have a food cache there somewhere, as they often head straight for that spot when they leave the chicks.

Having not been to the nest for several days, I'm vaguely anxious about the ravens. Further down the coast, I found discarded air-gun pellets, and Jóhannus told me that teenagers from a nearby village sometimes go there for shooting practice. Even after an overnight absence, I approach the nest with a degree of apprehension, and feel a wave of relief when I see that all three chicks are still there. But something has changed while I have been gone. The chicks are larger and more alert, lifting their heads and turning to inspect movement near the nest or on their skyline. Their plumage is silkier, with a bright sheen on their wings and those broadening black backs. They have the gloss of newly laid tar, the smooth perfection of feathers lengthening for a lifetime of soaring and tumbling on blustery draughts. Now they are beginning to stretch and flap their wings occasionally, a foretelling of power. Inside their nook they are dry, while I am wet and cold as I hunker down on the knoll. The fulmars are still on their perches above the cliff, but the rain has silenced their chatter. There is a deep calm about the gorge. The downpour has bolstered the streams flowing down from the mountainside, and on the ravens' wall there are three distinct waterfalls now, all of them at the seaward end of the cliff. Their splattering chattering fall into the channel below is a soothing white noise.

5

Walking on Water

'One day soon you will kill a whale. Yes,' he said, taking another sip of beer, 'I think one day soon you will kill a whale.'

'But I don't have the licence,' I said casually, as if it was just a bureaucratic inconvenience. 'Well,' my friend replied after a pause, 'you will at least help me kill it. I will call you when I'm going next time.'

It was two thirty am, but the northern sky still held the light on that endless late-June day. After a summer street party, I ended up with friends on a small fishing boat in the marina in Tórshavn's west bay. The boat swayed slowly, magnifying the effects of regular infusions of schnapps from a ram's horn cup that kept reappearing from the galley to be passed around our group. The alcohol, and tiredness compounded by the bewildering lack of darkness, made me wonder if it was me or the boat that shivered on the still water.

Later, in the little house in the middle of town where I was staying for the summer, I stared out across the channel towards the neighbouring island of Nólsoy. The eeriness of the colourless sky and sea mingled with the silence of the pre-dawn in a moment of stillness. I thought of my wife and children at home in England, doubtless asleep, and questioned again why I was so far away. And why I was drawn back again and again to these outcrops in the far North Atlantic. And I thought about whether I might kill a whale. The air was still and the birds were not singing. Even the geese in the neighbouring garden were not yet up and about. It felt as if the turning world had paused; it was the time of day when they say gravely ill people most easily slide into death. In this curious far-northern night-day, thoughts took on disproportionate strength, and ultimate truths seemed attainable. After a decade of visits to Faroes, something that was once unthinkable now felt possible.

I think back to when I was eight and we lived in Malaysia. I belonged to a gang of boys, all of us army brats constantly playing at soldiers. Sometimes we would arm ourselves with sharpened bamboo poles and venture into the jungle, where we believed there were wild pigs, which we convinced ourselves we were brave enough to hunt. We never actually found any and usually returned home dehydrated and covered in leeches, which we delighted in removing from between our toes by sprinkling them liberally with salt. As we never found any pigs to kill, we had to be content with simple patrols reenacting jungle warfare against the enemy – always the Japanese (rather than the Germans), whose invasion of Malaya was a relatively recent folk memory for our parents' generation.

One evening, playing outside a little way from our house, and on my own, I spotted a very large toad sitting in the grass. It may have been a bull-frog, but I remember its rich brown skin was covered in bumps and the call it made was a continuous *ritt-ur-ritt-ur-ritt-ur* growl, like the sound made by one of those old-fashioned wooden football rattles. It sat up high with its front legs extended and its head clearly visible above the grass, ignoring me as I approached. I had never been able to get so close to such a large toad before. Without pausing to think, I stooped down and picked up a half-brick lying by the side of the road and threw it. Perhaps I wanted to see how high it would jump. Unexpectedly, the brick landed squarely on top of the creature and I ran forward in my shorts and flip-flops to inspect my marksmanship. The brick had squished the toad's back legs so that they trailed uselessly, but the head and forelimbs were intact. Its mouth opened and closed, gulping soundlessly. I can remember clearly the feeling of revulsion and guilt instantly sweeping over me. The mangled amphibian was an unpleasant sight but I knew that it could not be saved. I picked up the brick and brought it down again on the gasping creature. It did not die, but squirmed and flipped over onto its back. The pale distended stomach stretched like a balloon, going up and down rapidly. Three, four, five times I attempted to crush the life out of it with the half-brick but still it gasped. Each time I raised the brick I became angrier and more sickened, squeamish at the moist mangled tissue. I began to cry, panic rising that I was failing to end its suffering. Finally the remains of the toad stopped moving, and there was no doubt it was utterly dead. I slunk home, my stomach tight. It was a sensation of pure guilt that I had never experienced, and something I was too ashamed to tell anyone about, even my friends. I had not only failed to kill it quickly like a proper hunter, I had destroyed something beautiful. In Faroes, these memories resurface, hard and unforgiving as the sheer forbidding cliffs.

I have never been squeamish about animal husbandry, and once dreamed of being a vet. My mother bred Siamese cats for showing, and we always had dogs too, so there were constant trips to the vet and the innumerable emergencies that accompany kittens and puppies being born. Almost all trips to the vet were my responsibility. I gave medicine, removed stitches from wounds, and my teenage years hold memories of cleaning up blood, shit, piss and vomit in all and every combination. I loved our animals and if they had to be put to sleep, it was me who stayed with them as they died. Killing something for food seems justifiable, but if I am unlikely to eat it, then I balk. At university I used to go clay pigeon shooting with a friend on his parents' farm. One late afternoon, when the mist was beginning to descend on the fens, a flight of ducks came straight towards us. I had the gun, and my friend urged me to take aim. I raised the barrel and realised it was an easy shot. But I didn't pull the trigger. 'What's wrong?' my friend asked. 'I just don't need to shoot a duck,' I replied. 'Well, don't tell my father when we get home,' he said. 'Or you won't be very welcome in the house again.'

While diving, I have met many whales and dolphins underwater in the Atlantic, the Pacific, the Caribbean, in the Indian Ocean and even inside the Arctic Circle.

Those encounters have felt as powerfully spiritual as any moment of my life. After thousands of hours spent underwater hoping for encounters with marine life, it frightened me that I no longer felt a moral certitude that I would not join in with a whale drive, even though I had always insisted to my Faroese friends that this was a line I could never cross. That line is still there, but becoming fainter.

Nólsoy is a gigantic bulwark protecting Tórshavn from the worst of the easterly winds. It could be a sleeping whale, a silhouette of gentle curves, humped and half submerged, bulbous and tapering. It dozes opposite the town, a fixed point in the endless skittering shadow show of cloud and current. Even from Tórshavn's old fort at Skansin right at the water's edge, the whole island frequently melts away, erased from the horizon by a magical shroud of mist and rain. But, often enough, there are days when Nólsoy glows, lit up by a low sun. Then, it hovers; a glowing spaceship between sea and sky. And in the small silent hours when the moon is full and rising above a tenebrous sea, I have found myself awake and alone, mesmerised by clouds racing above the island, chasing one another away and into the blackness at the edge of the world. It truly seems a floating thing, like Tír na nÓg and other mythical Atlantic islands.

Take the little ferry *Ternan* across the channel, and you reach a wide neat harbour lying on an isthmus, a low depression between the curving hills where brightly painted houses cluster together. Close to the tumble-stone breakwater, there's a neat white church with its door and eves painted emerald green. The crossing is only twenty minutes from Tórshavn, and in summer it's common for people to go to Nólsoy for a few hours for a party, or a concert at Maggie's bar. Some people choose to live on the island and commute to the capital to work. Others stay on Nólsoy precisely to avoid the faster pace of life on the bigger island. Tjóðhild Patursson is one of them, a willowy young woman with sea-green eyes who runs *Gimburlombini* (meaning 'the Young Female Lambs'), a cosy wood-panelled café in an old warehouse overlooking the harbour. It serves home-made cakes and doubles as the local tourist information office. Underneath the café is a boathouse where the rowing boat *Diana Victoria* sits as a memorial to the man who rowed it single-handed almost 1500km from Nólsoy to Denmark. In 1986, Ove Joensen took forty-one days to complete the marathon journey, his third attempt at the voyage. The first two attempts (1984 and 1985) both ended with emergency rescues by the Shetland lifeboat. Ove (afterwards nicknamed 'Ro-Ove') enjoyed brief fame, but no riches apart from a commemorative cup and the new bed he was given by one of his sponsors, a Danish furniture company. In typically Faroese manner, he said he would use his fame to raise money to build a swimming pool for the people of Nólsoy. The fund is still collecting, and the islanders hold a festival in Ove's name each August, although the aim now is to build a sports hall rather than a pool. Ove is not around any more. One night, a little over a year after completing his marathon voyage, while rowing back to the island from the small town of Runavík, he fell overboard and drowned.

'Ro-Ove' is not the most famous sailor to come from this small island. That honour goes to Páll Poulsen Nolsøe, now known as 'Nólsoyar Páll' (1766–1809). At the comparatively late age of 20 he went to sea, and rose to the rank of ship's captain during a career that took him to America, the West Indies, Portugal, England, France and much of Scandinavia. Returning to Nólsoy to marry a local girl, he began sailing for the Royal Monopoly. In operation from 1535 until 1856, the monopoly was originally granted to an individual – usually a Danish court favourite – in return for a fixed payment to be made to the royal exchequer. At one time, trading rights were given to merchants from the Hanseatic League, and the Danish crown even offered the islands to England's Henry VIII in exchange for a loan. The monopoly holder, or company, was allowed to charge a tariff on almost everything of commercial value, from feathers and sheepskins to whale oil and beer. They were also tasked with ensuring that there were foreign buyers for the most significant imports – especially woollen socks, which sold throughout Europe and were exported in bulk to the Netherlands. However, there was an understanding that the monopoly holder would treat the community fairly and ensure that essential goods never ran out. Profits were small, but even so, in an island nation beset by fog and rain and peopled by expert sailors, there was smuggling. Boats would call at Faroes with illicit goods to offload while pretending to be fishing vessels en route to Iceland looking for temporary shelter from a storm.

The monopoly warehouses and the tariff treasury are

still there, a tidy collection of ochre-red buildings on the Tinganes peninsula in Tórshavn, many of them still in use as government offices. In 1709, the monopoly passed from a family named Gabel back to the Danish crown (King Frederik IV), which decided that it now wanted a share of any revenue generated by the islanders. Tariffs were used to maintain government buildings, pay civil servants and employ a small garrison for defence.

Nólsoyar Páll was an extremely inventive man, using the knowledge he had gathered on his voyages to make significant improvements to Faroese boat design. Among the talents he brought home from his travels was a love of reciting poetry by Robbie Burns. Widowed in 1800, he remarried soon afterwards and moved to the fishing port of Klaksvík, Faroes' second-largest town. His ambition was to make sure that Faroes had its own fleet, in the hope that the trade monopoly would be abandoned. The monopoly administered law in Faroes, and among other restrictions decreed that extramarital sex was a criminal offence, and couples could not marry unless they had a certain level of income – measures designed to keep Faroes' population stable. In a way, such laws were an extension of the thirteenth-century 'Sheep Letter', which decreed that 'no man who owns less than three cows is to set up house on his own'.

Páll believed that free trade would bring greater wealth to the islands, and in collaboration with two business partners, asked for a loan from the Danish exchequer to buy a ship, a request which was denied even though the king's bailiff and the Royal Monopoly manager in

Tórshavn supported the idea. Refusing to be discouraged, Páll and his partners bought a wrecked hull at auction and rebuilt it as Faroes' first schooner. They set out fishing for the first time in August 1804, christening their forty-five-foot-boat, *Royndin Fríða*, meaning 'Beautiful Trial'. Other voyages involved taking coal from the small seam on Suðuroy to Copenhagen, and cargoes of Faroese sweaters and woollen socks abroad. On a return voyage Páll was successful in bringing back a smallpox vaccine to the islands. In Denmark, he had used the powdered scabs from a smallpox patient to inoculate one of his sailors. Rubbing the powder into a small cut produced a less dangerous reaction than the full-blown virus. This process, known as variolation, was used to inoculate the next person and so on, until they reached Faroes, where much of the population was successfully immunised.

Páll is also now known as the composer of the *Fuglakvæði*, the famous 'Ballad of the Birds', running to over 200 verses. The song was extremely popular, and subversive, because the Danish authorities are portrayed as predators, while the Faroese are smaller birds alerted to danger by the warning song of the oyster catcher. The oystercatcher – the *tjaldur* – is now Faroes' national bird. Its insistent cheeping call is the sound of spring and a constant accompaniment on any walk into the hills throughout summer.

Páll continued to campaign for free trade, and find ways to circumvent monopoly rules, and was several times charged with smuggling and other crimes. Just when it seemed as if he would get concessions from the king, his negotiations were interrupted by the 1807 outbreak of war between Denmark and England. In early September, the British bombarded Copenhagen for several days, killing almost 200 civilians and setting fire to more than a thousand buildings.

The hostilities were part of the wider Napoleonic struggle, and the British Royal Navy wanted to stop Danish ships becoming part of an alliance with Portugal and Russia, which would effectively enlarge the French fleet. The consequences for Faroes were dire, as during the British blockade of Copenhagen, essential goods, including grain, could no longer reach the islands. However, Páll lobbied the British Admiral, James Gambier, for permission to return to Faroes, and was given special dispensation to carry food back home. In 1810, the Faroese were then classified by the British as non-hostile and labelled 'Stranger-Friends' – a status later shared with Icelanders and Greenlanders. There would be an eerie echo of this diplomatic exception for Faroese ships by the British during the Second World War.

In spite of his protected status, however, during a voyage to Denmark in 1808 to attempt to get more barley for Faroes, Páll's ship was seized by HMS *Fury* and suffered damage while being escorted into Gothenburg harbour. Although Páll was initially imprisoned, he managed to convince the British to send him to London, where he appealed to the Privy Council on behalf of Faroes. Then, as the *Friða* could not be fixed, he was given a new ship, the *North Star,* which he filled with grain for the journey home. He set sail from London in mid-November and was never heard of again. The winter was especially harsh in the North Atlantic that year, and it seems most likely that his ship was lost in a storm, but many Faroese believed that skulduggery had taken place, and that his ship might have been sunk by a privateer hired on behalf of the Danish Royal Monopoly to silence him.

* * *

Tjóðhild cycles the short distance along the harbour road to collect flour and vegetables for her café when the ferry comes in. The bike originally had an electric battery to help with the climb back up the slight hill to the café, until Tjóðhild steered it off the jetty into the sea with its cargo of lemons and potatoes early one summer. 'It was quite a story here,' Tjóðhild explains with a smile. 'The battery was ruined, but I salvaged all of the vegetables and fruit.' Like several other younger people on Nólsoy, she returned to the island after studying abroad, and prefers its tranquillity to the bustle of the capital with all of its 20,000 inhabitants. Only around 200 people live on Nólsoy, all within view of the harbour and its dramatic archway formed from the jawbones of a giant whale. Pedestrians enter the village, Jonah-like, from the harbour slipway. The animal, probably a fin whale or even a blue whale, was not hunted, but found floating at sea near Vágar in 1895 and bought by two men from Nólsoy. The archway was originally erected in 1907, in honour of a visit by Frederick VIII of Denmark, knocked down by a lorry in 1957 and then cemented into its current position in 1975 for a visit by the Danish queen.

My interest in Nólsoy is based not on ocean giants, but on the island's colony of storm petrels, the smallest seabirds on earth. There is a man here who has been studying them for years – Jens-Kjeld Jensen, a Danish ornithologist. His house on Nólsoy is at the northern end of the village. Tjóðhild tries to call him on the telephone but there's no reply, and she says I can wait in the café until we find him. She offers me tea – raspberry, lemon or blueberry. I would rather have 'English Breakfast', but Tjóðhild and her colleague Barbara say they have no such thing. In a glass jar above the cake display, I spot something that looks suspiciously like a teabag, and ask what it might be. 'I don't know if you want that,' says Barbara. 'It's what my grandmother would drink.' I decide to risk it, and sure enough it turns out to be proper tea. 'We call this "*tee-oop-uh tay*",' Barbara explains, ferreting around in a cupboard to show me the box. Recognition dawns as I spot the red package inscribed 'Typhoo'. 'It came here during the war, with the British soldiers,' they explain. 'Along with Cadbury's chocolate. We don't have so much Danish chocolate here, everyone grew up on Cadbury's.'

There's still no luck tracking down Jens-Kjeld. The café is about to close, and Barbara says she needs to leave, because she has some orphaned lambs to feed. I stay for a little while, and Tjóðhild tells me more about her affection for life on Nólsoy, and how she values its peace and quiet. In summer, she runs activities for children on the little beach at the edge of the harbour, and she, along with Barbara and some other women enact plays based on the legend of the Scottish princess who is supposedly buried on the island. The story says that the woman fell in love with a commoner, and eloped to escape her father's wrath. Settling on Nólsoy, she believed she would never be found, but the couple (and their young child) were later apprehended by the king's men and taken back to Scotland. Happily, the monarch forgave his daughter because he was enchanted by his grandson, born on the island.

As Tjóðhild shuts up her café, I wander over to the other side of the village to see if there is any sign of life at Jens-Kjeld's house. It's a square, faded-yellow building, very much the shape a child would draw, complete with chimney set atop its orange roof. I knock, and after a time, a man with an unruly white beard and piercing blue eyes behind small wire-framed spectacles appears. He seems unprepared for company. I introduce myself, explaining that a friend in Tórshavn said that he had kindly offered to talk to me about the natural history of the island. 'Why didn't you come yesterday?' he grumbled. 'Er, I was only ever intending to come today,' I mumble. He stares at me for several seconds, before replying. 'I was expecting you yesterday, but you're here now, so come in.'

It turns out that Jens-Kjeld has mixed me up with someone else, and he gradually relaxes as he shows me around his study. There is a strong smell in the room that I can't quite identify. I suspect it has something to do with the dead kittiwake on the table by the window, one of Jens-Kjeld's taxidermy projects. The room is full of stuffed animals and too many birds to count, almost all of them provided by islanders who have found them dead and donated them to the collection. Facing me is the head and neck of an elegant whooper swan, and above it the head of a mountain hare. There are stuffed oystercatchers, guillemots, razorbills, eider ducks and shags. I see a hedgehog, and a skua, all of the gulls, a Manx shearwater and a storm petrel. There are puffins and a tawny owl, brown rats and field mice, even a raven with wings extended and a shiny beak that seems poised to strike.

Jens-Kjeld speaks a heavily accented mixture of Danish and Faroese, and for my benefit, English. He is wary of the outside world, and pessimistic about how development, especially tourism, may change the islands for ever. Behind the gruff exterior, he is kind, and passionate about everything in nature. Sitting with my back to one of several bookcases, I hear a distinct scuttling noise, and turn to see that my head is level with a box full of giant cockroaches. 'I keep them here to show Faroese children,' Jens-Kjeld explains. 'It's always interesting to see if any of them will be brave enough to hold one in their hand. They rarely see insects, and they tend to be nervous of them.' I can't help wondering whether holding a giant cockroach is the easiest introduction to the insect world. Everything here is testament to the forty and more years Jens-Kjeld has lived in Faroes. He, and his wife Marita, are obsessively interested in every aspect of natural history. Their website, and the numerous books they have written together, document everything from flies to rare migrant birds, invasive species of insects and the hundreds of species of flowers, ferns and fungi of Faroes. Jens-Kjeld is especially fearful about the possibility of rats, which could devastate the ground-nesting petrels on Nólsoy, and a recent worry has been the appearance of wasps around Tórshavn, which many people believe were imported in the turf used to surface the pitch in the national football stadium. After half an hour of chat, he tells me he wants to have a rest, but says he will go out later to the bird colony, if I want to join him.

It's almost midnight by the time we set out, and the village is deserted. Midnight doesn't mean much at this time of year, under the veiled sky. Darkness, softened by the candlelight glow of a sun that is barely below the horizon, will last just a couple of hours. Even if it was pitch black, I would be able to trail Jens-Kjeld by the scent of bird oil on his jacket. We pass a small walled garden where he points out several dwarf shrubs, willows and juniper trees, examples of native flora that he believes represent the original vegetation of Faroes, species eradicated from the lowlands by the ubiquitous sheep. He's interested in the idea of turning the nearby island of Koltur into a national park, without livestock, and watching to see which plants return to the landscape and thrive. The wind is as much an obstacle to trees as grazing animals, and although, thanks to the Gulf Stream, the weather is reliably mild most of the year, up in the mountains the climate has a mean monthly temperature below ten degrees centigrade. While the archipelago is roughly four degrees below the Arctic Circle (just over 300 miles south of it), about seventy per cent of the land area of Faroes is more than 200 metres above sea level. Up there, on the high ground the islands are defined as Arctic.

We follow a sheep track south from the village, skirting east around the humped shoulder of Eggjarklettar, the high point of the island. Jens-Kjeld aims to reach the bird colony in the brief period of twilight that occurs at around one thirty in the morning in the shadow of the mountain. Storm petrels come ashore to feed their chicks in underground burrows in the darkest hours, so as to avoid being attacked and killed by prowling seagulls and skuas. There is a cool wind tonight, and the sound of the sea echoes off the high ground.

At first the landscape is typically steep pasture, narrow rutted paths cut by the neat cloven-hoofed sheep that make living contour lines on the sloping ground. As we head further south from the village, the land is strewn with boulders, forcing us away from the lee of the mountain, until after almost an hour we reach Suðuri í Dølum, where a narrow grass plateau lies beneath the high rocky escarpment of Nýggjurðarberg.

The light is dim and the mountain seems malevolent, as if it has the power to dredge up spirits from somewhere deep underground. Thousands upon thousands of pale lumps of stone litter the ground, all of them about as big as a good-sized armchair, and a pall of mist hangs off the mountainside like a moving grey ceiling. The echo of the surf is a threatening soundtrack in the background. As we walk cautiously among the boulders, I am conscious of another sound, a low murmuring, burbling and grumbling. It is puffin voices, deep and warm, mingling with the wind. We carry on, and as we approach the headland of Bólstaður, the orchestra welcomes a new instrument, the low *brarp-brarp* of the male petrels, and then a higher-pitched contribution that goes *uhr-uhr-uhr-uhr-uhr-uhr-ick*. The English ornithologist Charles Oldham who studied them for years on the islands off Pembrokeshire, famously said he thought it was 'the sound of a fairy being sick'. If he had been alive fifty years later, I think he would have said they sound like the whining trill of a dial-up internet connection.

Nólsoy is home to one of the largest breeding colonies of storm petrels on earth. These tiny creatures weigh about twenty grams (half the weight of a tennis ball) and measure less than six inches long. They come to this island in huge numbers – impossible to count but there are probably almost a quarter of a million birds – to use this large boulder field as a ready-made nesting site. In spite of their small size, the 'stormy petrels', as they were once known, spend the European winter in the waters east of South Africa, or west, off Namibia, before migrating to Faroes to lay a single egg. They never come onto land except to lay, and both parents share the brooding. Probably because their lifestyle is so demanding, these tiny birds take a year off from reproducing every few years.

Hydrobates pelagicus has been called 'St Peter's bird', because it hovers inches above the sea, apparently 'walking' on the water by paddling its broad feet while holding its body above it with its uplifted wings. It is able to dance across the water and pluck the tiniest of crustaceans from the surface. But those seemingly magical legs are not strong enough to allow it to walk on land. Once on the ground it shuffles and stumbles, using its tarsi

– the long bones connecting the toes to the tibia – and its spindly legs are useless for digging. To nest it must find ready-made gaps between the boulders on Nólsoy, sometimes already occupied by bustling puffins. The birds can use a common entrance to the burrow, but once inside, the petrels will use their beaks to carve a side-tunnel too narrow for the barrel-chested puffins to access. Jens-Kjeld explains that fortunately the relative isolation of the petrel colony has meant that rats have not discovered the area.

For about an hour, the sky holds onto a trace of weakest watercolour blue, a uniform wash of light giving no clue of sun or moon. On the plateau, all I can see is the uneven ground below the gloomy mountain. If I crouch down low to listen to the petrels, the burbling coming from beneath the boulders disappears. The fact that they can sense me reminds me of looking for cicadas in the summer grass, a noise that invades the night air but dissolves like a receding rainbow as you run towards it.

Jens-Kjeld sets up a mist net between two lightweight poles at the edge of the boulder field, nearest to the cliffs. The mesh is fine and the whole upright construction looks very much as if we are preparing to play a game of badminton. He tells me to crouch down by the rocks. A few puffins potter about, their white chests visible in the gloaming. For some minutes we are alone with that curious orchestra, with occasional barking additions from the puffins which, like the petrels, become invisible among the boulders but can clearly hear or smell us. I am aware of the vastness of the ocean around the island. I feel its presence in the amplified sound of the wind, and the way the half-light bounces back off the surface of the water. The sea is darker than the night, a force that dwarfs the mountain and makes me feel as insubstantial as the birds. Standing on the edge of this small sliver of basalt, I cannot begin to imagine what challenges they face finding this place year after year, after travelling 6000 nautical miles all the way from the South African Cape. In spite of their size they fly fast, and one bird ringed in Scotland was in Faroes just twenty-four hours later, covering a distance of 650 kilometres. They can also live a very long time, with several individuals known to have survived thirty-five years.

Nothing happens for quite some time, and in spite of the proximity to mid-summer, I begin to feel the cold. I pull up the hood on my coat and sink my chin into my chest, burying my hands in my pockets. And then, against the sky, I detect a flash of movement. A colourless shape rapidly zigzags within inches of my head, and Jens-Kjeld nods silently in my direction. I can tell he is nodding only because his Father Christmas beard reflects the ambient light. The petrels appear with a rapid, jerky motion, more like a bat than a bird. Within minutes, there are a couple of dark shapes in the net. Jens-Kjeld picks them up gently in his large hands, and passes one to me to hold while he measures it. Up close, I can see its shining eyes and that extraordinary beak, glistening with oil and downturned at the tip. It has a tiny protuberance on the top mandible, which holds the nostrils and makes it part of the so-called 'tube-nosed' bird group. These little smudges of dusky feathers with their awkward walk and burbling talk also possess a keen sense of smell, and it's thought to be part of how they find their dens.

The bird flexes a perfect fan of charcoal tail feathers, made elegant by a narrow white band at the base. It is a tiny soft presence in my hand, giving off a strong stench of fish oil, which is immediately forgiven when I stare into those intense shining eyes. Periodically, it spews a dribble of glistening stomach oil, adding a polished sheen to its bill. Jens-Kjeld warns me the smell will not wash off my clothing, but I dare not alter my hold on the tiny creature, convinced that I will crush it if I flex my fingers even slightly. 'Throw it upwards' Jens-Kjeld advises, and I loft it skywards, anxious that my clumsy grip has somehow robbed it of the power to fly. I scarcely hear it go, hardly feel the weight release from my hand and sense rather than see a mere shadow against the muted sky.

Ravens V

Early June

Jóhannus has asked me to meet him at the ravens' gorge. He has a climbing friend who is a licensed bird ringer, and he is coming to examine the chicks and weigh them. I resent the intrusion into the nest, and worry that handling the birds will disturb the raven parents. I have become unreasonably protective of this isolated spot, and cherish my time with the young birds. At the same time, the chance of seeing them up close is too tempting to miss.

This is a dry day. Two of the mini-waterfalls have slowed again to a trickle, although the main cascade is steadily draining into the neck of the ravine. Things are ripening. The first heath spotted-orchids have flowered, standing just proud of the turf. They are newest pale pink, wide agape and displaying their striated lips, incongruously vivid and exotic in the matted grass at the cliff edge. The curving green leaves below the flower heads show brown marks, like liver-spots on aged fingers. Mushrooms have started to appear, too, tiny wax caps no more than a few centimetres high. When I arrive, Jóhannus is already at the sheep pen with two men, Abraham Mikladal and his son Bergur. Bergur and Jóhannus were the first men to climb Geituskorardrangur, a 121-metre vertical sea stack off the west coast of Vágar. Among other firsts accomplished in Faroes, they have also ascended over 300 metres to the needle-top of Trøllkonufingur (the 'Troll's Finger'), an expedition with two other climbers which took forty-eight hours. Today, Bergur plans to go down to try to catch the raven chicks, while his father waits at the top. The forty-metre raven cliff is barely a challenge.

In my customary spot on the north side of the gorge, I watch as Jóhannus and Bergur busy themselves with affixing their climbing ropes to the rocks above the south wall. Abraham, a man with a calm and serious demeanour, has brought his bird-ringing equipment and a set of portable scales, the kind of small hand-held things people use to weigh their luggage before a plane journey. He explains to me that he has been collecting data on Faroese ravens for several years, and that he will pluck some small feathers from the chicks' underbellies which will be sent to Germany for DNA analysis. The only way to sex a raven chick is by blood from the shaft of the feather.

Bergur walks backwards, abseiling down the steep sheep-rutted ground, and descends the cliff quickly and smoothly while Jóhannus supervises the rope. Hanging in mid-air beside the nest, I watch him gently scoop up the first chick, and then a second, and place them in cloth bags, which are tied loosely at the neck. He fastens the bags to a rope line, which Jóhannus then hauls upwards, slowly and carefully. I hurry over to watch the chicks being weighed. The young birds are still and calm in their unfamiliar surroundings, not calling or crying out at all. Holding them firmly, Abraham takes the first chick from its bag and deftly removes a couple of small feathers, placing them in numbered vials. He then swiftly affixes a metal ring to one leg and records the chick's weight.

Abraham passes me the other bag to hold, while he finishes working with the first raven. He says I should keep it out of the direct sunlight, so that it doesn't overheat. The sun is shining, although the early summer temperature today is only about fifteen degrees centigrade. However, this is warm, compared to the insulated chill of the gorge, and I suspect that the ravens could soon stifle in the cloth. I can feel the blind shape of the raven through the bag as I place it on the grass carefully, watchful in case it wriggles and rolls down the sloping ground. It is an odd thing to know that the chicks are out of the nest and in my care, if only for a few minutes. My hand hovers gingerly above the bag while it ripples and flexes as the baby starts looking for a way out. Abraham works quickly and explains that he wants to make sure they suffer as little stress as possible. I hand him the bag so that he can weigh it. The smallest bird is just over 1200 grams, and the largest slightly more than 1400. As Abraham suspends the third bag on the scales, the chick pushes its head out through the opening. It swivels its head left and right fiercely. The beak is remarkably sturdy, a powerful tool, and when closed tight it reminds me of a monstrous carnivorous tooth. At the base of the beak are bushy bristles, like a cropped horse's mane. They are not feathers, not soft or fluffy, and they extend halfway down the gently curving bill. They are part of the raven's unbirdliness. Where the two halves of the beak meet there is a pucker of bare skin, a hinge of flesh that allows the bird to stretch its beak wide. Inside, a strong tongue flicks up and down. It's startlingly pink, the exact shade of stewed rhubarb. But I am transfixed by the bold shining eye of the raven. The iris is a ring of sky blue. It shines bright and evokes power.

Abraham tells me he will send the feathers to the laboratory, and in a month or so will get news on the sex of the birds. Bergur, meanwhile, is still suspended at the end of the rope, waiting to replace the chicks one by one in their nest. The whole process is all over in less than ten minutes. While the others head back to the farm track with the climbing equipment, I linger for a few minutes to watch the nest. The chicks resume their customary position, lined up side by side, and show no sign that anything unusual has happened today. I relax, glad they are back where they belong.

6

A Sheep Letter

At this time of year, the dry-stone walls around the coastal villages come alive. Starlings in their thousands have built their summer nests inside nooks and crevices and the walls begin to sing. The shimmering adult birds fly through tiny chinks between the stones and vanish in the blink of an eye. I like to creep slowly up to the walls to peer inside, hoping to catch a glimpse of a snug little grass-lined chamber where the chicks are waiting. There are walls like this around Kirkjubøur, on Streymoy island, one of the oldest settlements in Faroes, and once the seat of ecclesiastical power in the islands. The living centre of the settlement is an imposing wooden farmhouse tucked behind and slightly above a stone church, both perched by the shore of the fjord. Once upon a time, the church was further from the sea, and there are remains of buildings on an offshore islet that were originally part of the village before the Atlantic crept in. A thin ribbon of about two dozen homes is the southernmost village on this, the largest island.

Tórshavn isn't far away, but it's on the opposite side of this narrowing tail of land, hidden behind the 300-metre hulk of Kambur mountain. Offshore, dominating the view, are the two small islands of Hestur and Koltur. Local people translate the names as 'The Mare' and 'The Colt'. It's a commanding spot. Look north up the fjord and you catch the cliffs at the southern end of Vágar, while to the south you glimpse the larger bulk of Sandoy. The currents are strong, and all kinds of things are carried ashore. Villagers see seals and orcas in the narrows between here and Hestur, and recently a fifteen-tonne blue whale washed up on the beach close to the church.

The church is named for St Olav and was built, they say, in 1111, the oldest place of active worship in the country. In spite of the Faroes' modest population, this has been home to thirty-four successive Catholic bishops, the last of whom, Ámundur Ólavsson, died in 1538. Just before his death, Faroes was annexed by Denmark, the existing churches were made Lutheran, and Catholic-held land confiscated by King Christian III.

Alongside St Olav's church sits a twelfth-century cathedral, roofless and windowless. But neither the little white church nor the high stone ruin say as much about Faroes to me as the farmhouse. The grass beside the path to the front door is bordered by a blue-whale jawbone embedded in the ground. The whole building exudes a creaking weathered warmth that could only come from ancient wood. A thousand years ago, in this land devoid of even medium-sized trees, the log cabin structure was floated over the sea, towed behind a boat all the way from Norway. The logs that make up the walls are cylindrical, but it reminds me of the model houses I made of ice-lolly sticks when I was a child. Inside, at each end of the logs, you can find tiny holes, small enough to have been made by a thin nail. There's a single hole at each end of the first log at ground-floor height, which slots into the adjacent log at ninety degrees. This log is also marked with a single hole, while the next pair up bears two holes, the next three and so on, allowing the craftsmen to match each joint and reassemble it without instructions. It's the first Scandinavian mail-order kit house. More remarkably, the people who live here are the seventeenth generation of the same family who took over the farm in about 1550. It may be the oldest home continuously inhabited by the same family in Europe.

Like half of the farms in Faroes, Kirkjubøur is on 'king's land'. Once the seat of the bishop of Faroes, this estate used to stretch northwards up the coast past the village of Velbastaður and east over the mountain to Argir, to the outskirts of Tórshavn. Originally leased to tenants who paid rent in the form of wool, butter or other produce, these king's farms are now leased from the government for a nominal or peppercorn rent, a relic of the system introduced when the Danish crown confiscated episcopal lands during the Reformation. Getting to grips with Faroese land systems isn't easy. For a start, land is measured in *mørk* – pronounced *murshk* – and one *mørk* contains sixteen *gyllin*. One *gyllin* is twenty *skinn*. An added complication is that a *mørk* on one island is not equal in size to a *mørk* on another. I have asked many times for an explanation of the *mørk*, but it remains unclear how to measure it. Until the late nineteenth century, it was used as the basis for land taxation and as a measure of the wealth of the outfield, but the units of *mørk*, *gyllin* and *skinn* seem not to have an intrinsic value. When buying a share of outfield today, it is important to know how many sheep will be sustained on the *mørk* you acquire; on Skúvoy it might be as low as eight, while on Mykines you can have twenty-six sheep per *mørk*. On Stóra Dímun they can have thirty-four, and in the east of Vágar it could be forty-five. There is probably a connection with the ancient *merk* used in Scottish measures, especially in Shetland and Orkney, where one *merk* of land would support a single cow.

The current farmer at Kirkjubøur is Jóannes Patursson, and he keeps sheep, horses and a small herd of Highland cattle on his land. By historic right, he also owns the grazing on the offshore skerry called the Trøllhøvdi ('Troll's Head'), ten kilometres across the water and close to the northern tip of Sandoy. It's not entirely clear how this small islet came to belong to the farm, but the farmer has a theory. In a rich gravelly voice, cured, in his words, 'by too much tobacco', Jóannes says he believes the farm was given the islet as compensation for having to row government officials from Kirkjubøur all the way over to the east coast of Sandoy. The settlements on Sandoy were once confined to the wide bay at Sandur, on the far south-western side of the island. Rowing or sailing over to the main island of Streymoy therefore meant a long slow haul up the west coast. The easier, more direct route was to the north-east tip of the island – in direct line of sight from Kirkjubøur. As there was no village there, the

Kirkjubøur men would have to make the return trip as well, after being summoned by a lit beacon when they were needed. 'It could also be,' Jóannes muses, 'that the bishop of Kirkjubøur wanted the islet so the village would have some fowling sites when times were hard. Sandoy has many good bird cliffs on the other side, but here around us we don't really have any.'

Jóannes and his family are surrounded by family heirlooms and reminders of their long lineage in this place. In the formal sitting room, portraits and photographs of ancestors line the walls. Next to a grand lacquered cupboard are paintings of his great-great-grandparents Guðny and Jóannes, and close to a small side table bearing a silver tray and a candlestick are formal portraits of his great-grandparents Páll and Jeyja. His grandparents Malan and Jóannes are there too, in charcoal drawings near the piano brought from Denmark in 1865.

Jóannes has an endless fund of stories about the history of the farm and his family, which he tells with great pride. He's the great-grandson of Jóannes Patursson, a farmer-poet who founded two of Faroes political parties. There's a bust of the elder statesman in the farm's old *roykstova* or smokeroom. Above it, and up a short, extremely narrow carved staircase, is a neat loft room lined with ancient books, with a small desk and a chair with a sheepskin seat. It's a cosy space lit by a tiny window and a skylight at the roof apex. They say the bishop of Faroes penned the nation's oldest surviving document here in 1298. It's called *Seyðabrævið* ('The Sheep Letter'), and bound inside the *Kongsbókin* ('The King's Book') – a velum law journal preserved in the national archives in Tórshavn. Its main purpose is to set out the rules and regulations for shepherds, and the compensation payments due for lost sheep. The pages are thin and covered in spidery ink, and the thick leather cover carries the patina of something handled thousands of times, stuffed in and out of a travelling bag by the island lawmaker and carried from island to island in all weathers by rowing boat. In one margin, there is the black-ink hieroglyph of Earl Haakon (the thirteenth-century ruler of Norway), a stylised 'H' with an extra vertical line up the middle in the shape of a spear.

The *roykstova* is sturdy, impervious to the wind and rain that lash off the fjord with dependable regularity. In 1772, this was the only part of the farm to be undamaged when a massive avalanche swept down from Skorðarnar, the high rockface above the old cathedral. Although it's part of the modern Patursson home, the *roykstova* is now preserved as a museum, full of old farming tools, a cast-iron stove and the paraphernalia of whale hunting. The room smells of woodsmoke, and standing inside you feel like you are sharing the air with the thousands of people who have cooked and eaten here over the centuries. Along one wall is a long narrow dining table, still used for large gatherings and big enough for eighteen people. It's pale and worn, scratches and dents in the surface rubbed smooth by generations of elbows and hands.

This table was not always a table. It was once a hatch cover on the iron-hulled three-masted steamship *Principia* which was carrying cargo between Leith, Dundee and New York when a fierce fire broke out in the forward hold on 16th November 1895. Eight men were on watch in the small hours when the blaze started, and six of them had no choice but to jump overboard to escape the flames. As the alarm went up, a ship's lifeboat was launched, which managed to save two of them. Meanwhile, those left on board tried desperately to slow the flames by throwing the remaining supplies of coal overboard. Five days later, afloat but severely crippled and still smouldering, the 2749-tonne *Principia* was hoping to make land in Scotland. Captain Richard Stannard was sailing blind – the smoke from the forward hold obscuring everything in front of him. The ship struck rocks off the west coast of Sandoy and sank. Stannard and most of his twenty-eight crew died, along with their single passenger, Harry Jackson of Dundee, who was on his way to America to take up a job as a draughtsman in Chicago.

At Kirkjubøur farm on 22nd November, knowing nothing of the drama that had taken place on the far side of Sandoy, Jóannes Patursson (our farmer-poet-politician) despatched a young apprentice named Jógvan Joensen to take two horses across the mountain trail to Tórshavn. As he reached the high ground overlooking the fjord, he spotted driftwood and raced back to the farm. Thanks to the absence of trees in Faroes, any timber was very highly valued, and salvaging it was an essential key to survival. In rough seas and a biting wind, Patursson set out in a rowing boat up the fjord along with his brother Sverre, young Jógvan and three other men from the farm. A little way up the coast, close to the spot called Gamlarætt, they saw a man clinging to one of the ship's half-submerged cargo hatches. With difficulty they prised him off the wood and brought him back to the farm and the warm *roykstova*. Patursson instructed his apprentice Jógvan to take off his clothes and get into one of the bunk beds with the unconscious man to revive him with his own body heat. The boy, who was only fifteen, refused, saying he was scared, and so Patursson stripped off and huddled up with the drowned sailor to save him from fatal hypothermia. Some hours later, the man revived and told them his name was Heinrich Anders of Rostock in Germany. He was eventually able to tell the Paturssons that he had been adrift for about fifteen hours, and had originally been clinging to the hatch with another survivor, the ship's sole passenger, Harry Jackson. Anders had given Jackson his life vest but the other man was too weak to hold on in the rough seas and was torn away by the waves. His body was later found north of Gamlarætt. Two other drowned sailors – one of them, Captain Stannard – eventually washed ashore on Vágar, carried north by the fierce westerly current.

Some weeks later, Heinrich Anders arrived in London, where he visited the shipping offices of the Arrow Line, owners of the *Principia*. Afterwards, he reported that he left the meeting in fear of his life, believing that the ship's owners had over-claimed on the insurance for the boat, having been paid an inflated value for the cargo on board. He also said that none of the ship's regular crew had been on board for the fatal voyage, and that many people suspected that the ship had been deliberately scuttled as part of a fraud.

In July 1936, a visitor arrived at Kirkjubøur. It was

Anders, and filled with emotion, he sat at the table in the *roykstova* and wrote in the Patursson guestbook, '*Now, I am sitting again on the plank that saved my life forty years ago.*'

* * *

The old village path to Kirkjubøur, from where young Jógvan spotted the flotsam from the shipwreck, is marked with stone cairns, vital guideposts when the mist descends. From the western side of the valley, between the hills, there is a clear view across the fjord to Koltur and Hestur. Koltur, the second-smallest island in Faroes, covers only two and a half square kilometres. Only uninhabited Lítla Dímun is smaller. Koltur looks like a giant skateboard ramp, its northern end a towering sugar dome peak almost 500 metres high that sweeps down with a dramatic curve to the flat land in the middle of the island. The ground then rises again gently to Fjallið, Faroes' smallest official 'mountain' (101 metres high) at the southern end. Bjørn Patursson, uncle to Jóannes at Kirkjubøur, lives on the island with his wife Lúkka and a small herd of sheep and cattle. Once there were two farms and as many as six families on this small green scoop of land, but now Bjørn and Lúkka are the only permanent residents. There are two surviving modern farmhouses on the east coast and everyone knows that they were home to the last two families from Koltur, who didn't speak to one another for over twenty years. Bjørn and Lúkka now live in one of them.

Bjørn acts as a guardian for the island. A keen naturalist,

he keeps an eye on the puffins and the black guillemots, the oystercatchers and the Arctic terns, all of them safe here as the island has no cats or rats. Bjørn also helps preserve an ancient farmstead a little way along the east coast from his farm. The island was the home of a famous boat builder, a man named Niklas Niclasen, who made 350 rowing boats here before he died in 1991 at the age of eighty-two. The farm dates from before the sixteenth century and is made up of a dozen low stone-built buildings, including Niclasen's boathouse, along with sheep pens, a byre, and the ubiquitous *hjallur* – the open-sided Faroese meat-drying shed – all nestling together close to the island's very short stretch of grey-sand beach. The old farm settlement is called *Heima í Húsi*, and in winter storms massive waves cast white clouds of spray higher than the turf roofs that make it blend into the surrounding pasture. I slept alone under the eaves in the old farmhouse once, inside a cosy traditional alcove bed with a sliding door to keep the draught out. Late at night it was utterly black inside, and the wind and the rain were banished in sight and sound.

Before potatoes were widely grown in Faroes (from the mid-nineteenth century), they grew six-row barley here on Koltur, picking it green, so that it didn't wilt and rot on the stalk when the autumn rains came. The barley ears were dried in the small stone houses called *sornhús* over a low fire made of peat. Life was never easy anywhere in Faroes, but here even the peat had to be brought in from another island.

One bright clear June morning, I watch golden plovers strutting along the southern end of Koltur, picking tiny flies off the seaweed left behind by the tide on the basalt shelf at this lowest end of the island. Bjørn tells me proudly that his sheep are clever enough to come down to the shore to eat seaweed. The rocks are warm to the touch, a rare day when there is no wind and the sea is free of chop. The foreshore shelves are decorated with bright white lichen, crackled like a raku ceramic glaze and making fantastical patterns on the basalt. They form Rorschach shapes resembling islands and amoebae and stingrays and knights on horseback. Directly opposite, I look towards the uninhabited north end of Hestur, just a bit more than a kilometre across the sea. They say a young man named Magnus used to swim across the channel, helped along by the easterly tide from the headland where I'm sitting, to rendezvous with his lover, the daughter of one of the farmers on Hestur. Hours later, the westerly tide would carry him conveniently home again. One evening, he made the swim and found her father standing on the shore with an axe. Magnus was swept away with the tide and never seen again.

One summer's night, I climb alone to the west side of the high point of Kolturshamar. The cattle are up here, some sheep, and quite a number of snipe who fly high and fast at my approach, their wings pushing the air through their outer tail feathers to make a hypnotic *huhuhuhuhuhuhuing* as they rise into the evening sky. Bjørn has made a fence to stop the livestock going around the flanks of the mountain, slopes so steep it's hazardous for man and beast. Climbing over the sheep fence to get higher, I reach the sharp line of a vertical basalt ridge that breaks up the green dome of the peak. Like a soaring fulmar I can see all the way down the sloping ground to the little farmhouse, where Lúkka gave me richly fermented *skerpikjøt* with bread and tea for dinner. There is a feeling of utter isolation up here in the fresh clean air. I clamber cautiously around the mountainside towards the eastern edge of the dome, and see that the drop into the fjord is sheer and intimidating. I carry on a short distance but the wind is picking up and I am utterly alone and out of sight of the farmhouse. There are no lights visible on the opposite shore, and I am suffused with a sense of dread, my mind filled with images of sliding down the damp grass and over the edge into the swirling tide race below. This end of the island is an impenetrable castle of rock rising vertically from the water. I think of the dead sailors from the wreck of the *Principia* being swept past this spot in the wild darkness of that winter storm. If I fell, the idea that no one would ever know what had happened to me is at once depressing and yet somehow thrilling. I have a strong sense of my own insignificance. Being one stumble from certain death is enough to make me squat on my haunches and scrabble crab-like back to the less precipitous face of the mountain.

* * *

There is no boat link today between Hestur and Koltur. But a ferry goes from Gamlarætt close to Kirkjubøur every day, even though the single settlement on Hestur now has only fifteen permanent residents, none of them under fifty. My friend Óluva's parents live there, and her father, Magnus, who is in his eighties, still farms. Óluva and her sister go over regularly to tend their own sheep, to plant potatoes and especially to help him with the haymaking in July or August, depending on the weather and how well the grass has grown. Magnus leaves the house by six am to cut grass to make the most of the long drying hours in a summer day. He returns in time for breakfast with his wife Fríðbjørg. I am invited for *skerpikjøt* and sliced cheese served with the round buns known simply as *bollar*. Afterwards, I follow Óluva on a short walk to the fields on the sloping land at the northern edge of the village. She shows me the building containing a small village swim-ming pool, built in the 1970s with the aim of making sure everyone on Hestur could swim. It was a good idea at the time, but there are no children here now to learn. There is not even a village shop. Groceries can be ordered and delivered by the ferry from Gamlarætt, which calls at Hestur on some of the crossings between Streymoy and Sandoy. For foot passengers there is a dedicated bus service which meets each ferry and takes passengers back to Tórshavn.

We walk past fields where the grass has already been cut and piled waist high. A patch of cloth is tied across the top of the ricks and tethered down with pegs in the ground at the four corners like a tiny tent. It's not to keep the hay dry, but to stop it blowing away if the wind picks up. Beside us the fjord is smooth, but the power of the channel between Hestur and Streymoy is still evident: the surface is mottled with deep shadows made by the undercurrent and patterned with swirling eddies.

Magnus has a small petrol mower, but mostly he uses a wooden-handled scythe on the uneven ground. The cut grass lies across the field in neat lines where it has fallen. We gather it and hang it on the sheep fence, turning it into a green wall. We let the breeze do its work for a few hours, then spread it thinly and widely across the shorn field, maximising the surface area of hay that receives the sun and wind. As we work, the air is filled with the piping cry of the oystercatchers, and they, and I, keep time to an ancient beat. I am pleasantly warm in the sun. This is a timeless moment, and reminds me of days in my childhood on a farm in County Down when my cousins and I played among the hayricks in the field next to my aunt's house. Today, on Hestur, we work until all the grass has been spread out before we have lunch, more *skerpikjøt*, cheese and some sliced carrot and cucumber. Magnus is strong and fit and I ask if he has ever eaten green vegetables. 'No, not really,' he answers shyly. He's not alone in that, and many of my younger friends also stick to a diet of meat and potatoes, with vitamin D provided by whale blubber, which was enough in the old days to prevent rickets. Rhubarb is commonly eaten, and kohlrabi, but it's quite easy to avoid vegetables altogether with Faroese meals.

It took me a while to get used to that most traditional form of Faroese food, the fermented and dried lamb or mutton called *ræst kjøt* (pronounced like *rast-tjiot*) and *skerpikjøt* (sounds like *shush-puh-tjiot*). It's not an immediate winner with the faint-hearted outsider, but it's a staple in many households, and I have been offered it at breakfast, lunch and dinner as well as in sandwiches and as a snack. Quite regularly it is the aroma that hits you when you enter a Faroese home, a sign that a traditional meal is being prepared. Almost every home still has its *hjallur* – the meat-drying shed close to the house, with at least one side made of open wooden slats or laths to allow the wind to blow through onto the meat hanging inside. Fish (predominantly cod or saithe) is also wind dried, usually hung outside under the eaves of the house or in the *hjallur* in pairs tied together by the tail.

The *hjallur* is a temple to meat. Dimly lit and eerily silent, it will have whole carcases and legs turning gently in the breeze, and perhaps some sheep's heads staring out from nails on the walls. Men show off their *hjallur* with pride, and it is a sign of welcome to be invited to go and inspect it in the company of your host.

It is the North Atlantic wind and the unusually temperate climate that has allowed the Faroese culture around fermentation to develop. It is a process that connects the land, the livestock, the elements and the people. Fermented lamb, fish, pilot whale, beef and poultry dry-aged in this way develop a unique *umami* flavour – the so-called fifth taste – after salty, bitter, sour and sweet. Fresh meat is hung in the *hjallur* straight after the sheep are slaughtered, and men always argue about who has the best drying shed and can produce the best meat. The direction of wind combined with the air temperature during the slaughtering is critical. If the sea is rough and the wind strong, it will make the air more humid and this in turn will affect the speed of desiccation and the taste that develops as the meat ferments. Just as wine producers need to know how sun and soil affect the quality of their grapes, the Faroese must understand how seasonal winds and humidity will impact the taste of the cured meat. When hanging the meat, great care is taken to prepare the carcase cleanly with no nicks and tears in the muscle. Any irregularities in the surface are an opportunity for a fly to settle and burrow into the flesh and lay eggs. A good farmer visits his *hjallur* every day in winter to check for flies and scrape any eggs or larvae off the meat with his penknife. Another old trick is to place the lamb's carcase over a barrel of water or have a stream of water coursing through the *hjallur* in a channel in the floor – because flies won't lay their eggs above it, knowing that the fatted maggots will drop to the ground when they hatch. The meat gradually acquires a surface bloom, a fine striation of colours as bacteria colonise the surface, slowly turning it into a palette of delicate blue and brown, copper green and bronze, deepening into shades of charcoal.

In simple terms, *skerpikjøt* means 'dried meat'. In reality, the process is complex and relies on the North Atlantic autumn to produce its regular cool temperatures of between eight and twelve degrees centigrade. Any warmer and the hanging meat (which is not salted or smoked) will begin to decompose and rot. Any cooler and it will simply freeze and not ferment. These temperatures allow the bacteria to do their work and the fermentation process to begin. After hanging for a few weeks, the fresh meat is slightly moist and known as *visnað*. It can be eaten at this stage, especially the meat from whales, geese, seabirds and fish, along with some gravy made from melted intestinal sheep's fat, though not so much mutton and lamb. Then comes the dry-aged phase – *ræst* – where it develops its characteristically pungent and bitter taste. In this phase – typically approaching Christmas – the thinner cuts of meats, such as the ribs, are eaten after being boiled or roasted. After at least six months, lamb and mutton are properly dry – *turt* – and brought to the table and sliced into pieces like any form of jerky. Some people claim that the real *skerpikjøt* state is only reached after more than a year of wind-drying and fermentation, although in recent years anything older than six months has been classified as such.

Faroes' unique combination of low temperatures, reliable wind and lack of insects has allowed the skills of fermentation to flourish. Fermentation – in biological terms the production of energy from nutrients without oxygen – is an ancient practice found throughout the world, crucial to the preservation of food before refrigeration became available. Similar to the process that creates yoghurt, the chemical reactions at work in Faroese traditional meat preservation are still not fully understood, but at the most basic level they involve bacteria partially digesting the meat as it steadily loses moisture. Typically, lamb will have a moisture content of about seventy per cent when it is hung straight after slaughter, but thirty per cent or less when dry aged in a *hjallur*. It is this water activity and the proliferation of bacteria (probably transferred to the carcase from the farmer's hands) – at first aerobic varieties and then anaerobic later in winter – that produce *skerpikjøt*. At least 600 species of bacteria are thought to be involved in producing the distinctive 'high' flavour of Faroese meat, but fewer than one hundred have been positively identified in the laboratory. In simple language the *skerpikjøt* is 'cheesy', but the strength of the flavour varies tremendously according to how long the meat has aged and the temperatures in which the fermentation took place.

It is very important not to confuse the smell and taste of Faroese food with anything 'rotten'. Peter Panum, a Danish doctor who visited the islands in the mid nineteenth century, later described *ræst* fish and meat as 'half-spoiled' with 'an abominable odour and an unpleasing, mouldy appearance not infrequently occupied by maggots'. I have often been warned not to repeat the slur.

* * *

After drying, the hay needs to be piled into mounds and then crammed into a tarpaulin, which is tied into a secure bundle for the journey back to the village. Magnus uses a handcart, a wooden contraption like the old luggage trolleys they once had at railway stations. The large bundles are far wider than the base of the cart, and they must be manhandled carefully into position and then pulled back to the house, where the *hjallur* is ready for this year's supply of hay. Inside, it is a typical farm outbuilding, containing assorted pieces of old furniture, piles of timber, a few wooden barrels and, in one corner, a modern chest freezer. Óluva says it is full of meat, including whale. There are a couple of formica tables and some lengths of rope, as well as some large blackened objects hanging from nails behind the door. They resemble giant shrivelled prunes, but they are old buoys called *grindakíkar*, made from the dried stomachs of pilot whales.

Now, it's time to throw the new hay into a stack inside the *hjallur* as a winter food store. I take a turn with the fork, its smooth wood shiny and silky from years of handling. It's hot work and the air fills with the dizzying notes of summer grass released by the sun and the sea breeze. The colours of the strands are as complex as their scent, and in one handful I can pick out filaments of sea green, rich copper, cactus blue and swan's-bill orange. Motes of hay rise into the air, and the afternoon light shining through the slatted rear wall of the old barn turns them into a rich ochre cloud, a miniature cosmos of whirling particles.

Ravens VI

June

The ravens are standing and turning in the nest now. The chicks are big enough that when one of them stretches its wings, the others react, shuffling and scootching on their bellies in their bowl of sticks. The weather is a degree or two warmer, and there has been no rain for just over a week. The two smaller waterfalls have dwindled to nothing more than damp patches on the basalt, and even the main river-fed stream has slowed to a trickle that sticks to the rock. It no longer has enough force to arc out over the water below, and when the wind blows offshore the gorge seems to trap its own silence.

At midday, the car thermometer reads sixteen degrees centigrade in Tórshavn, and out on the cliffs the sub-arctic flowers are making the most of the summer. When my eye filters out the prevailing green of the mountainside, there is a lot more colour now, mostly confined to the steep upper layers of the walls of the ravine, and out of reach of the sheep. Dainty Arctic mouse ears with their distinctive double-lobed petals speckle the heath close by my own roost, paper-thin flowers springing from a tangled mat of foliage that forms little islands in the grass. At the heart of the flower, there are lime-green starfish-shaped anthers. The long stringy stems are virtually leafless and covered with a thousand bristles that catch the dew.

On the rock walls, there are several clumps of northern rock-cress. They spring impossibly from the vertical cliff, extending one long stalk outwards over the precipice as the elegant porcelain-white flowers seek the sun. Up close, the petals are thicker than the delicate mouse ears, and have a rougher feel, as if they have been dusted with microscopic crystals. I have found the convoluted unfurling flower heads of mountain sorrel too, noticeable for their slightly vulgar shades of arterial pink.

With the ravens' increased activity, I am finding it harder to leave the gorge unvisited for a whole twenty-four hours. There is an air of expectancy here. Often I return for a second visit during the long slow twilight. Well after sunset, the sky stays pale and there is no true darkness. Under the calm of that sleeping sun, I hear the chicks murmuring in the nest. It is a low *gurr-gurrk*, perhaps as close as a raven gets to sounding pleased, and deeply comforting to me. I doze in the grassy hollow, and wake to find the fjord has become a smooth wash of magenta, a mirror to the sky.

7

The Whale Drive

I'm sitting on a bench close to Jacobsen's bookshop in the middle of Tórshavn when my phone lets out the low chiming alert for a text message. I ignore it for a moment, enjoying the August sunshine and studying the three old maple trees in front of the nineteenth-century turf-roofed building. In this prime spot, I can also see an even larger beech, standing proudly on the patch of grass outside the *Løgting*, the islands' parliament. Trees are what I miss most in Faroes, and these three are some of the largest in all of the islands. Sometimes I just sit and admire them for a few minutes. Apart from the so-called 'national forest', a small plantation of mostly willow and birch near the art gallery in Tórshavn, it's rare to see decent-sized mature specimens, certainly never on the mountainsides, because of the wind, and hardly ever in the outfield because the sheep mercilessly crop any new growth before a sapling can establish itself.

When I finally look at the phone message, I wish I hadn't. It's Jóhannus saying that I need to drive as quickly as possible to the far north, to a fishing village called Hvannasund, where there is a good chance that a *grindadráp,* a pilot whale drive, will happen. He warns me that if I leave it too late the traffic will build up and I might not get there in time to see the kill. 'Do I really need to leave straightaway?' I reply, playing for time while the news sinks in. Yes, he answers, because he has advance warning from a friend on a boat who's involved. He's not going, but he says a public announcement will be made on local radio once the hunt supervisor is fairly certain the whales can be beached. Then men will flock to the village to help them haul in. Anyone who helps will be entitled to a share of the meat.

The route means driving towards the island of Viðoy. It's at least ninety minutes away, close to the furthest point accessible by road from Tórshavn. The meandering fjord-side route out of town leads me across the narrows between Streymoy and Eysturoy by roadbridge. After crossing Eysturoy island, I take the six-kilometre-long sub-sea tunnel to the major port of Klaksvík, following winding roads north and east to negotiate more road tunnels into Hvannasund.

It isn't the journey that makes me hesitate. It is the prospect of finally seeing a pilot whale hunt at first hand. The very idea of the whale drive and the killing of these elegant animals dominates so many conversations about the Faroe Islands. In spite of repeated negative publicity over what they call the *grind* (which rhymes with 'wind'), I have met very few Faroese who believe this ancient tradition should stop. Those who do are mainly concerned about the health consequences of eating the meat, which is known to be contaminated with mercury, in common with most marine mammals worldwide as a result of industrial-era pollution. Large fish like tuna, sharks and the biggest feeders at the top of the food chain are especially heavily contaminated, because they accumulate all the toxins in the smaller prey they have consumed. At the top of the food chain, these pollutants and heavy metals pass into the tissues and fat and are therefore not excreted. In pilot whales, mercury is a particular concern as it affects the development of the nervous system in human foetuses and may compromise the immune system and mental development.

I have discussed the idea of the *grind* for several years, accepting the arguments that it is seemingly sustainable, that the animals are not endangered and that outside opinions on the morality of killing these oceanic dolphins are all too often clouded by sentimentality and false information. My personal concern about the slaughter is due to what I know about high cetacean intelligence, their social networks and the increasing evidence that they can communicate with one another in more sophisticated ways than we previously imagined possible in any animal other than ourselves. Outside Faroes, the very mention of my affection for the place frequently brings quizzical glances and sometimes hostility from my friends in the world of marine conservation. People who know nothing else about the islands will often simply say, 'They kill whales, don't they?'

During numerous visits over several years, I had never been in the right place at the right moment to see a whale hunt. It's not something that can be predicted, and because the animals are only driven inshore when conditions are right, a successful drive can never be guaranteed, even at the optimum times – during high summer and early autumn. Even so, I had long felt that watching videos of whale drives online and reading other people's accounts of what they had seen was not enough. My journalistic instinct has always been to witness events and practices personally before pontificating on them. If I was going to join in the debate about whether or not this thing was sustainable and moral, or a barbaric historical legacy, then I needed to see it for myself. It seemed somehow dishonest to take a stand over the rights and wrongs of the issue if my knowledge remained theoretical, or based on third-party coverage. And yet, on this sunny day, I hesitated. Diving with cetaceans all over the world has provided me with some of the most valuable wildlife encounters in my life. Swimming with humpbacked whales in Turks and Caicos and diving close to them in Ecuador remain vivid memories, while meeting dolphins underwater in Seychelles and Ireland had been a virtually spiritual experience.

I have never met a pilot whale underwater, but a few hundred miles north of the Arctic Circle, I once went in search of orcas. Socially, they are very similar to the long-finned pilot whales of the North Atlantic, though larger, and famous for being able to take any other marine mammal as prey. In weak December daylight, I floated face down in a dry-suit, mask and snorkel, staring into infinite depths. In Norway's Tysfjord, the water had the delicate sepia tinge of fine China tea and a sepulchral gloom that was strangely calming. There was a stiff south-west wind whipping up the surface into small white crests all around me. Adrenalin made me oblivious to the temperature, though I knew the water was only four degrees centigrade. I also knew that I was alone and floating in the path of a school of killer whales, an animal which many marine naturalists consider the ultimate ocean predator, regularly preying on seals as well as much larger whales and dolphins. It is the most widespread of all cetaceans and found right at the edge of the pack-ice at both the North and South Poles. A mature male orca can reach almost ten metres in length, with a dorsal fin well over one and a half metres high. Like many other dolphin species, the social construction of their groups, rather like in elephant society, relies heavily on the leadership and knowledge of mature females. We know now that female orcas live into their eighties (much longer than males) and at about forty they experience menopause – seemingly an evolutionary trait that allows mature females of certain species (including elephants) to share 'childcare' with the younger generation, and pass on knowledge. We know too that their brain is four times larger than our own, and in terms of brain weight to body size the ratio appears to be the same as in a chimpanzee, something that corre-lates with what we know about orcas' capacity to learn. Intriguingly, the world's orcas are divided into several distinct sub-groups, some of which feed exclusively on fish, while others, the so-called 'transients' are much more adaptable in their diet, and potentially more aggressive.

In Norway, I had been assured that the orcas had never shown any interest in people as prey. Floating in that dark water and waiting to see if the orcas would come close enough for me to see them was undeniably thrilling, and provoked a mixture of high excitement and true trepidation. I had been dropped into the water by a small RIB, which had motored off to some 500 metres away, so as not to distract the orcas. I felt very alone. After a minute or two, I became conscious of something moving in the deep. It was a lone herring, the fish that brought the orcas into the fjord to feed. Seconds later a larger – much larger – cylindrical shape came out of the shadowless deep. It was a piebald giant, and I felt as helpless as the fish.

The Greeks called the orca 'the dolphin killer', and the Latin name *Orcinus orca* connotes the underworld god Orcus and translates as 'the whale from the realm of the dead'. In Norway, the orcas I saw were chasing herring, cooperating in packs to herd them into the depths by circling and frightening them into tight shoals. They achieve this by exposing their lighter-coloured bellies to the fish in the black water. Then, with the fishes packed into a dense swirling vortex, the largest orcas fan the shoal from close quarters with their tail flukes, creating a shock wave strong enough to damage the herrings' swim bladders. The dazed, uncoordinated fish can then be picked off and eaten one by one. Again and again, I watched these giant living submarines glide by me in the water. One day, an enormous male about three and a half times my length swam towards me. He paused in his journey, fixing me with a soul-deep eye, and then swam in a full circle around me to get a better look, probably using his sonar to investigate my internal organs as well. His bulk and clear physical power were mesmerising, and I found myself holding my breath. He could, in a flash, have taken hold of me and dragged me down or simply bitten me in half. But, holding his eye with my gaze, I realised that we were studying each other intently, both making an assessment about what we saw, whether it was a threat or a meal or something new to our respective consciousness. I had a powerful conviction that we were no less than equal. He was not just strong and dangerous, but graceful and knowing. And he was at ease and unhurried in that cool dim realm where he was king.

Like orcas, pilot whales are Odontocetes – toothed whales – as distinct from species such as humpbacked or blue whales, the filter-feeding giants with baleen plates in their mouths that sieve through seawater for small prey. The Odontocetes use their teeth for catching and killing their food, which in the case of orcas can be any other animal in the sea, from great white sharks and baby whales to seals, squid and herring. Pilot whales are rather gentler in their habits, specialising in catching deep-water squid with small peg-like teeth. In the family of oceanic dolphins, only the orca is larger. Known scientifically as *Globicephala melas*, due to their distinctively rounded head and jaw, they have been nicknamed 'potheaded whales'. It's just one of their common names; in the Hebrides they were known as *caa'ing* whales, perhaps because they were seen to 'call out' to one another. Generally, they fall under the catch-all of 'blackfish', which includes both long- and short-finned pilots as well as orcas and their smaller cousins the pygmy killer whales.

Pilot whales have neither the power nor, in my view, the grace of the orca. A study of their vocal calls has found that they share similar styles of communication with orcas, but even so, we do not revere them, perhaps because we are not afraid of them, or because we don't recognise them as especially beautiful. They don't breach and frolic as extravagantly as many dolphins, and they have never been made familiar through wildlife documentaries or displayed in captivity. Their diet is confined to fish and squid, and they live a mostly invisible life in the cool waters of the North Atlantic. Their biology is not well studied, and official estimates of their numbers are imprecise, though it seems likely there are hundreds of thousands of long-finned pilot whales. The whales that enter Faroese waters seem unaffected by human interaction, or at least unaware of the dangers of visiting, and the numbers killed have been fairly consistent for several hundred years.

Contemplating the *grind* on this sunny day, I fear not only that the spectacle will be personally distressing, but also that it may change my view of, and relationship with, Faroes. Watching this happen might unleash an emotional response that I fear I can't control. I don't want to become estranged from these people and this place which now feels like a home.

As I drive, I half hope that my journey will be interrupted, expecting at each turn in the road that a traffic jam will stop me reaching the likely whaling beach in time. I am already halfway to the north when the radio news bulletin confirms that a hunt is underway. Speaking via his mobile phone, the local sheriff comes on air to explain where the drive will try to land the whales. The whole process is tightly orchestrated, and specific rules are in place to minimise the danger to the fishermen and the shoremen and to ensure that the whales can be killed swiftly and their meat processed efficiently. Each island has a list of nominated beaches where it is legal and safe to drive pilot whales ashore. They must have a sloping area of sand, onto which the animals can land and where the hunters can steer their boats as close as possible. Then the sheriff warns that because his district has already had several successful hunts this summer, the community has taken the decision to distribute all today's catch to a neighbouring island.

I drive slowly, keeping to the speed limit, still curbing my prospects of getting to the area where the hunt is underway in time to see any actual killing. But nothing blocks my progress, and the expected rush of other vehicles dashing to the same destination completely fails to materialise. The final tunnel cuts through the heart of Toftaknúkur mountain. Entering into that unlit space requires concentration and an awareness of how far it is until the next passing place. In the gloom, I imagine the weight of the mountain pressing down from above. The basalt walls are misshapen, blasted into angular lumps that cast confusing shadows under the car headlights. The darkness stretches for two kilometres until the wormhole ends and the small circle of daylight at the exit grows bigger. I feel as if I am crossing into a different dimension. Here, my world will change.

The tunnel brings me onto a road high above the fjord between the northern islands of Borðoy and Viðoy. Then, there is a spectacular view over Hvannasund, sitting at the neck of a narrow sound. A thin strip of neat houses lines the hillside close to a small jetty, along with some fish-drying sheds and a red-roofed church. On this bright day, the sea is calm, and the steep mountainsides are a rumpled green cloth textured with the rippling tones of late summer grass. From my vantage point, in the shade of Toftaknúkur, a saddle in the mountain lets the sun light up the other side of the fjord, creating a stripe of bright gold above the village. Below me, a road causeway just a couple of hundred metres long joins the two islands, and turns the bay into a cul-de-sac. It is the perfect place for *grindadráp*.

From where I'm sitting, there is at first no clue that anything might disturb the scene. But, with binoculars, in the far distance I begin to catch flashes of white spray crackling the surface. Slowly, almost imperceptibly initially, the splashes become more obvious, and I can make out a line of small boats, more than twenty of them, abreast and low in the water. Soon, in front of them, I see the shining backs of the whales arching through the slate-coloured water. The movement of the animals is fast, the dives shallow and frequent, as they snatch racing breaths. They are just ahead of the flotilla, the noise of the engines pushing them forwards and ever closer to the shallows at the neck of the sound. From my position high up on the bank of the fjord, five or six fast-shifting shapes at a time are visible for a split second above the rippling water. It moves like oil, seeming to fold in on itself as the streamlined bodies push it aside. I know that for every pilot whale I can see on the surface there may be three or even four below. By my count, there are perhaps twenty or so in the pod, with at least two calves tucked in close to their mothers' sides. But then a few hundred metres away, I spot another group. I begin to hope that this splinter pod might break away and double-back past the boats. But as the fjord narrows like a funnel and the water becomes shallower, the two groups merge, and it is clear that there are many more, perhaps fifty whales fleeing from the noisy chase. To get a clearer view of the hunt, I drive down and across the causeway and park on the road above the church. Here, the men are gathering, all with knives at their belts, waiting with a dozen stout ropes and metal hooks in their hands.

The leader of the group is easily five metres long, blue-black skin shining like a London taxi in the rain. Driven from behind by the action and noise of the little motor boats, he comes onto the shingle first, other pilot whales crowding around him and lining up with their flanks touching as they roll in the shallow water, unable to stabilise their bodies as they form an unwitting queue for execution. The men beach him, and all the others, on the narrow shingle and rock foreshore in front of the houses. At water level, it is a small flat area, no more than fifty metres wide, a colourless little beach framed by two small concrete slipways. And there, below the well-kept houses, within sight of the village church with its red corrugated roof, the slaughter unfolds in front of me. Jaunty fishing boats, one banana yellow, another with a lipstick-pink cabin, a collection of dinghies, even tinier inflatables and one larger tugboat all crowd towards the shore making a wall of engine noise and banging hulls to frighten the whales ahead of them. Four men stand holding the thick rope with the metal grapple, in reality a blunted hook, the *blástrarkrókur*, which one of them pushes into the blowhole on top of the first one's head. And then they haul, leaning back against the straining tether. They are in jeans and short rubber boots, knitted sweaters and hoodies, nylon football shirts and anoraks.

To quell my own rising distress, I begin deliberately to observe the detail of the scene, as if my brain is simply a recording device, a camera and a tape recorder that will store the truth of everything in front of me for later. I am aware of the great thrashing splashing body of whales in the shallows, and of men calling out to one another. It is brutally orderly, a rapid, grisly team effort with death at its core. There is no teenage bravado, no cowboy yelping or evident bloodlust, just barked instructions. I watch men in high-vis vests with the word *grindamaður* printed across the broadest part of their backs. The 'whale men' are the ones who carry the short spinal lances called *mønustingari*, the most modern of the killing tools, introduced as a humane measure to replace the old harpoons and long-knives. They are inelegant weapons, just a slim shining shaft with a lozenge shaped blade ten centimetres long resembling the leaf of a hornbeam tree. The tip is for piercing the skin and blubber, and the sharpened rounded edges will efficiently sever the spinal cord. The blade sits in a sleeve, a cup which steadies the tip against the skin, a hand's width or more behind the blowhole. Immediately after severing the spine, a sideways motion allows the curved sides of the blade to cut all of the major arteries carrying blood to the brain.

Balancing on some boulders protruding into the shallows, I am within a few feet of the big male when they drag him onto the sand. Tears silently well up in my eyes as seawater splashes over my boots. I look around to see if anyone else is upset by what is happening. But everyone else is focussed on their task. The few spectators, older men and a handful of women and children, stand chatting calmly, watching the slaughter from a few metres away as if the villagers were simply herding sheep.

In seconds he is almost out of the water, arching his tapering flanks and showing the delicate grey pattern of his throat, as neat as if it had been stencilled on with a spray paint-gun. It forms a ghostly imprint against the blackness of his head and sides. Rolling onto one side, he exposes the long belly slit concealing his penis. That intimate view, the indignity of that unnatural pose, makes me look away. I am instantly reminded of how sexually playful all of the dolphin species are at sea. I can also see the scratches on his belly and the grazes on the underside of his fins where he has scraped against the rocks on the shoreline. Aside from the abrasions and minor cuts, he is vigorous, and utterly alive. His tail rises high to form a perfect crescent, neat flukes raised into the air higher than any of the men on the strand. I hear a single short squeal. Pure streamlined muscle power makes him buck and fight against the rough shingle, pebbles and grit sticking to his unblemished belly with its super-smooth skin. This rough shore is a most unnatural deathbed for an animal that dives 600 metres to chase squid in the sea. At his side, I see the long thin pectoral fins, much longer than my arms, but against that elegant smoothly moulded body they look like foolish little boomerang-shaped wings. And there, closest to me in that famously melon-shaped head, is one eye, tiny, beady and unblinking. The local sheriff, the *sýslumaður,* is first to reach him. He is an important man with the power to deny permission for a whale drive, though that is rare. Up to his knees in the surf, he holds the lance like a spade and places it rapidly without hesitation behind the blowhole. A swift pump of his elbow and the cutting edge slides in and down as easily as a syringe. The whale stiffens. His tail makes a flicker-quick slamming jerk against the water and it is over. Another man with a long, long knife runs forward into the troubled spray and slices deep into the sides of the head, deep butcher's cuts to reach the carotid arteries and bleed out the carcase. And so it ends. The glistening skin is rent by a deep gaping wound and inside, the bloody anatomy of blubber and muscle and bone is fully displayed. He is no longer a pilot whale fighting to return to the deep. He has become a silent lump of flesh waiting to be carved up for meat. But all around, the shallows are staining. It is a deep-carnation emulsion, richer, so much glossier and more vibrant than the red roof of the nearby church. This is oil paint crimson, living cadmium spreading onto the rocks and high up the legs of the men. It forms into a water cloud twenty metres out across the neck of the sound, opaque and uniform, picking up the afternoon light and holding onto it, glistening and alive where it meets the inky water of the fjord.

The killing goes on for another twenty minutes. By then, forty-five pilot whales are lined up on the gravel. A tall athletic young man stands panting in the shallows, soaked from head to toe with seawater in the cool air. He has diamond-blue eyes and eyebrows and hair the colour of sun-dried hay. At some stage he has wiped the back of his hand against his forehead to leave a smear of scarlet against his pale unlined skin. It is so subtle a mark, so elegantly casual and understated, that it might have been meticulously painted on by a make-up artist. His hands are scarlet with blood, which has run from the tip of his hunting knife back over the handle, between his long strong fingers and into the cuticles around his nails. The broad blade is thick with sticky jam-like gobbets and there are patches of red across his sweater and around the belt on his sodden jeans. Now, wading through the painted water, he moves among the still corpses, tying a hawser around their tail stems, assembling them into groups of four or five to be towed back across the bay to the wharf on the other side. The largest of the fishing boats backs towards the beach, and he passes the rope to the two men in the stern. It begins shuttling back and forth, and in a short time the motionless torpedo carcases are fastened to stanchions on the far side of the narrow inlet.

Perhaps half an hour later I cross over to the wharfside and find myself alone and looking down into the glassy water at the bodies. Tethered in groups of three or four, they float at the surface, in still water not discoloured here with gallons of blood. There is no more bleeding to be done. Tails curved like brackets bump against the old lorry tyres attached to the concrete wharf as fenders. The tyres match the black skin of the whales but they are dull, ridged and patterned by their tread, while the whale skin is smooth and shines like glossy latex. Deep incisions run down either side of the each animal's neck so that barely attached heads nod grotesquely in the gentle swell. As they flap in time to the wavelets the marbled muscle beneath the skin and fat shines in the oily water. It glistens like the moist flesh of a freshly sliced pomegranate.

In some animals the teeth are visible, widely spaced and small in relation to the melon shaped skulls. These are not teeth to be afraid of, but stumpy and yellowing, like glimpsing into the mouth of an aged beggar on the street. A clump of seaweed, a funeral wreath, drifts over one trio of pilot whales, and settles at the neck of a baby nestled between two adults. In life the infant would never have slept on its side like this, nor been so utterly still. At sea, most cetaceans sleep with one eye open, half of their brain awake while the other half rests, so that they can consciously breathe.

Over at the beach the crowd has already dispersed and the villagers have resumed their daily routine. Here, on the rain-slick wharf there is just a lone fishermen in neon orange overalls sheltering in the lee of a nearby shed. He tells me he is waiting for news of a lorry, equipped with a crane-arm and winch, coming from the neighbouring

island to transport the carcases for butchering and distri-
bution. A call on his mobile phone confirms that the lorry
is having to wait its turn in the single-track tunnel. The
sun has gone, obscured by a featureless cloud which hides
the mountains all around, and steady fine rain is falling. I
look back up the fjord in the direction of the open sea. The
scenery is restored to its postcard simplicity, and now the
church roof is the only blood-red flash against the green
hills. And then at the surface, just metres from the beach
I see a familiar curve, the dorsal fin and arching back
of a living whale. This lone survivor is cutting back and
forth across the channel, making rapid dives, searching or
waiting for the others in the group to return.

* * *

The whales have come again. This time to Vágar, and the
killing is over by the time I reach the port. There they
are: seventy-five pilot whales lined up in two parallel
rows, skin brightened with the steady morning drizzle.
Unusually, there is also one bottle-nosed whale, a species
that sometimes gets caught up in a pilot whale drive. It
will taste just as good.

After the slaughter, the immediate job of opening a
trapdoor of skin and blubber through which the entrails
spill has been done. This will let the carcases cool and stop
the meat from spoiling. Each black body is first numbered
with Arabic numerals crudely incised into the skin with
a knife, usually on the head between the eye and the jaw.
The whales are then measured from eye to anus with a

specially calibrated rod – the *grindamál*. Then, another number is more precisely carved into one of the pectoral fins, this time in Roman numerals. This is the whale's value in *skinn* – officially 50 kilograms of meat and 25 kilograms of blubber. In reality, because the way the animals are measured is an estimate of their volume based upon length, it averages out at about 38 kilograms of meat and 34 kilograms of blubber. That's because older animals get rounder and fatter but do not grow beyond a certain length.

I am looking at whale number 42, and on the fin it says VII. This means it has a value of seven *skinn*. Amid much chatter and bustle from the men on the quay, the butchery begins, and soon the head and the tail are the only recognisable parts of the whale still attached. The stomach and intestines are piled up on the jetty as the men flense the chunks of meat and blubber. It carves easily. Pieces will be allotted to those on the verified list in a meticulously laid-down order. The rules have changed over the years, but whale meat was long allocated to the boatmen, the community, to the crown, to the poor and to each man according to his role in the hunt. Those regulations remain, and there is even a rule about how much compensation should be paid for losses incurred during the drive – from damage to boats to broken spectacles or lost dentures. To this day, the largest whale always goes to the man who spots the school at sea first and raises the alarm. Usually, anyone who attends the drive on a boat or gathers on shore to help haul and kill will receive a share. The community focus, and value of the *grindadráp*, within this tight-knit society cannot be underestimated.

Today, in the place where the whales died, there is no disguising the charnel debris left by the butchery. Severed dorsal and pectoral fins lie on the jetty alongside the piles of intestines. The whales display their teeth, their guts, their bones and joints and skulls. Here and there, in that sleekly domed head, the one-way mirror of an open eye glints beer bottle green. Ribs and spines show through the thin layer of meat left on the carcase, and, where the head meets the body, the crucial first cervical vertebra – the atlas – is exposed. Between this vertebra and the next is a gap about five centimetres wide. This large, triangular arched bone has a hole through its middle, a tunnel through which the whale's major blood vessels reach its brain. Cutting through this gap deprives the whale of oxygenated blood and it is paralysed and unconscious within two or three seconds.

Official government advice is that when making the lance thrust into the whale, the point of the blade must be placed slightly more than a hand's width behind the blowhole, angled a little towards the tail. Once the blade has penetrated the spinal cord, it must be flexed left and right to ensure all blood vessels are severed. The larger the whale, the larger the gap, and the thicker the blood vessels. This is why the blade is sharpened on the sides as well as at the tip. Its width (forty-seven millimetres) is calculated to fit into the open angle of the vertebral ridges protecting the spinal cord.

In human beings, and most other land mammals. the blood to the brain is carried through the carotid arteries on each side of the neck. These large arteries carry blood to smaller branching arteries which are connected to different areas of the brain. In pilot whales the carotid arteries feed more directly into the spinal canal, dissipating blood to the brain through a network of blood vessels known as the *rete mirabile* – the 'miraculous net'. This extremely fine network of blood vessels is a two-way heat-exchange system, and it allows diving mammals to separate the blood flowing to the brain from the blood in the rest of the body and limbs – meaning they can keep the brain functioning while other parts of their body cool down significantly. Many animals use this system. Birds do something similar with the blood supply to their feet, and African gazelles use the miraculous net to keep their brain at a safe temperature even when exerting their muscles as they sprint across the hot savannah to escape a cheetah. In whales, the *rete mirabile* also allows oxygen-rich blood to be supplied to the brain slowly, helping to avoid the problems human beings experience when swimming at depth – principally the bends.

When pilot whales are killed, there is a second stage to the blade work before the butchery of the meat begins. Within seconds of the spinal lance doing its job, a long knife must cut deeply into the sides of the 'neck' and empty the carotid arteries of blood. This violent bleeding is not about killing the whale, it is simply about removing the blood from the meat so that it doesn't spoil. As we've seen, it turns the water crimson. Bays filled with dead pilot whales (and sometimes white-sided dolphins too) are an abiding image of Faroes which provokes intense emotion.

It has made the islanders targets for environmental and animal rights activists over the past half-century. Where once the whales were speared and stabbed as they crowded into the shallows, much research and effort has gone into refining the slaughter to make it quicker and more efficient. The blowhole hook is blunt and designed to fit into an opening above the 'nostrils' of the whale, and not be gouged into the flesh itself. Inside the blowhole opening, there are two chambers, and the hook does not obstruct the breathing. The new spinal lance was introduced after 2011, designed specifically to allow the blood vessels within the cervical spine to be cut as quickly as possible. Nonetheless, for anyone unused to witnessing the slaughter of mammals, the sight and sound of the process is shocking.

The naturalist Kenneth Williamson described a large whale drive he witnessed in 1941; 'Men and beasts seemed inextricably confused in the bloody, quaking turmoil of the sea. The spear-thrusts sank deep, viciously biting into blubber and flesh. Within a few minutes of the start of the kill the harbour was a scene of gory madness and carnage, and the strong smell of blood filled the air.' The preeminent Faroese painter Sámal Joensen-Mikines created some of his most powerful, dynamic paintings depicting the whale drive. 'In these pictures I have found a valid expression for everything I was striving for,' he said. 'They are my vision, as well as a synthesis of the nature of Faroes, and man's will.' Sometimes seen as a metaphor for the Second World War, the theme of the *grindadráp* is another aspect of the artist's preoccupation with death.

He produced around fifty *grind* paintings, capturing the swirling mass of men and whales, the arching spurts of blood and the grace and beauty of the animals all at once.

If the *grind*, and the painting of it, says something about the essence of what it means to be Faroese, then it's worth noting that Mikines was sometimes ambivalent about the spectacle. He said in an interview in 1955 that 'the pilot-whale drive is indeed a barbarous practice, a relic of a heathen way of life, when we see men driven forward, possessed with psychotic fury, wild and besotted with blood. The only thing I can say in its favour is that the killed whales have been harvested from time immemorial, and you have to believe that the Faroese have learned to kill these animals in the most humane way possible.'

They have killed and eaten whales here for more than a thousand years. In 1298, Faroes' oldest written document, the Sheep Letter, decreed that among other things 'men who drive a whale ashore and do not themselves own the land above the shore; are to be given a quarter share'. The Faroese have doubtless been killing whales for even longer than written history reveals, just as people did in Shetland and Norway and Ireland. In the days of small wooden rowing boats, it was a hazardous enterprise. While out fishing, the men would carry things like castoreum and juniper leaves to throw into the water if a whale of any kind came too near to the boat. It was believed that these pungent items would keep whales away and protect the fishermen from being swamped or crushed. Written records of how many whales have been killed, and on which beach and how much meat they yielded, date back to 1584. That list, showing the date and place and number of every pilot whale slaughtered, and the weight of the meat distributed, may be the oldest continuously documented record of a human relationship with another species. As of early 2020 the total number of pilot whales ever caught over 425 years in Faroes was approaching 264,000 animals.

Pilot whales were caught often enough that for many years their skulls were commonly used to build walls around gardens and vegetable plots in Faroes. A Danish government official making a report on the *grind* in the eighteenth century referred always to the number of whales 'who laid their bones'. The providential nature of pilot-whaling is clear, 'the good God has richly and roundly blessed the land with whales…even in places where never before whale-killings have taken place (God give the inhabitants grateful hearts).'

Apart from its original essential value as food, the practical value of the pilot whales – and historically, the larger species too, is obvious. Whale skin was used to tie oars to thwarts, and as a generally hardwearing long-lasting material. Whale stomachs were tanned and used as buoys and containers for anything from lamp oil to wool, and many homes still have them tucked away in a shed or in a barn. A rib could be laid horizontally on the grass at the top of a cliff and used as a smooth runner for the rope attached to a man who was collecting birds' eggs. At Mykines, a set of whale ribs was used as runners for boats on the steep slipway. Pilot whale bones from Faroes were exported to Scotland to be ground up and used as fertiliser, many of them ending up on the Lincolnshire potato fields. Fresh pilot whale bones were also used as fuel for fires to save on wood. We did it too. Oil from rendered blubber was exported as a valuable lubricant. Not only was it resistant to freezing but it could also be used where purity and high viscosity were essential, in rifles, watches and intricate machinery. In the First World War, British infantry battalions were using ten gallons of whale oil per day to rub on the soldier's feet for the prevention of trench foot.

Counting marine mammals is notoriously difficult. The North Atlantic Marine Mammal Commission (NAMMCO) claims that there are at least 750,000 long-finned pilot whales (*Globicephela melas*) in the central and north-eastern Atlantic. In the eastern Atlantic around Faroes, there are estimated to be at least 100,000. If, as some biologists estimate, pilot whales reproduce at a rate of around eight per cent each year, then the Faroese catch is well below one per cent of the population, and should be sustainable. But killing any marine mammal, especially a cetacean, has become a fraught topic of debate.

Ethical questions arise from the particularly high levels of cetacean intelligence that test our moral judgement. If, as we believe, they communicate in a sophisticated way with one another, does it mean that they are especially prone to emotional distress during slaughter? For those of us who see whales and dolphins as creatures with close to our own levels of intelligence, and even revere them as having some kind of spirituality, this is hard. Every Faroese person I have ever spoken to about whale drives – virtually every Faroese person I know – will argue that pigs, cows and sheep are also intelligent, and that they see no special case to be made for pilot whales. In the old days people simply called pilot whales *sø-kvæg* – Danish for 'sea-cattle'. Having seen whales killed since they were very young children, they are no more upset at the idea than most people are about eating other warm-blooded animals. They are adamant, however, that any slaughter must be quick and efficient, and they are dismayed at the idea of animal cruelty.

In 2014, Pamela Anderson, (the actress and former *Baywatch* star) visited Faroes to add her voice to an anti-whaling campaign by Sea Shepherd. She labelled the *grind* 'barbaric', and urged the Faroese 'to make more sustainable choices about their diet'. She highlighted the fact that not only is killing pilot whales unacceptable for her, and for the organisation, but that their meat contains heavy metal and other 'persistent organic pollutants', including mercury. This is something the Faroese have known for many years, and government health advice is widely publicised, warning women of reproductive age and children that they should avoid pilot whale meat altogether. Official Faroese health guidelines state that pilot whale meat contains around two micrograms of mercury per gram and no one should eat more than 200 grams of whale meat per week, and no more than 200 grams of whale blubber per month. Pilot whale blubber contains relatively high levels of polychlorinated biphenyls (PCBs) and DDE (Dichlorodiphenyldichloroethylene), derived from the pesticide DDT. All of these chemicals are known to be toxic. Extensive medical studies are ongoing to measure the effects of these pollutants on people's general health.

Pamela Anderson was asked publicly if she thought that Faroese people would be doing less harm to the planet if they bought all of their food from the supermarket, which would mean they were increasing their consumption of industrially farmed and grown produce, and increasing the amount of packaged food that is shipped and flown to the islands. It was a question neither she nor anyone else could really answer. One Faroese argument is that when they kill pilot whales – which are driven ashore if they are spotted and not 'hunted' – they are eating meat that is 'local' and wild, from animals that have led an entirely natural existence until the day of their death. In moral terms, that seems arguably better than the life of a pig or a cow that has been fed antibiotics, kept indoors, possibly in a small pen, for its short existence.

I have lost count of the number of young Faroese men who have told me that they now join in with *grindadráp* precisely because of the campaign by Sea Shepherd. They say it was something only their fathers and grandfathers did, but when foreigners came here and said they should abandon something that was an intrinsic part of their culture, then it became important to learn how to kill a whale. Now, they turn out to help when a school of *grindahvalir* is spotted. 'It is part of who we are,' my friend Hilmar says. 'The whales saved us many times in the old days when the sheep all died of cold. Who knows what can happen in the world? One day we may have to fend for ourselves again.'

Kenneth Williamson summarised the role of the pilot whale drive in an article for the *North Western Naturalist* in the 1950s. 'It is only natural that such a remarkable phenomenon should have made an ineradicable mark on the material culture of the Faroese. To the observer from abroad the grindadráp must seem one of the cruellest forms of hunting in existence. But this is the only way to kill these whales successfully, and the conditions of life among the islands are such that the *grind* – like the sea fowling – remains a vital source of the country's meat supply.' Williamson's assessment is, of course, outdated, but many of my Faroese friends still consume whale meat as a significant proportion of their diet. Other foods are indeed available at high cost, but their provenance is not necessarily more ethical, and their production arguably less sustainable.

I have not been in the water with a long-finned pilot whale. They live in female dominated groups, and they are long-lived, similar in lifespan to an elephant – over fifty years for the males and longer for the females. An adult female pilot whale will be almost four metres long and weigh somewhere between 600 kilograms and just over a tonne. The male can reach over seven metres, and weigh over two tonnes. Like other large-brained animals, pilot whales reach breeding age relatively late, with females bearing their first calf at about nine years old, and males not breeding until they are well into their teens. They gestate for twelve months, and spring and summer is the peak time for mating, the season when they come closer inshore to shallower, calmer water. That is also when they are frequently found near Faroes, and when they are most often driven ashore and killed. Since 1584, almost sixty per cent of the whale drives have happened between May and September, with more than forty-three per cent in August and September. There is, however, no 'season' for whale catching; it can happen at any time of year, weather permitting.

In Faroes, many of my friends own guns and they always carry a knife when they go out walking in the mountains. At some stage, before I was welcomed into the seasonal cycle of sheep collecting and slaughtering, they would ask me what sorts of things I had killed, and how I feel about whaling and hunting seabirds. They were incredulous that I had little experience of such things. When I explained that I had killed rabbits, pheasants and once even a deer, all animals my dog had chased and failed to despatch, they were reassured. Broadly, a man is still expected to know how to kill. However, they listen politely when I express my reservations about the pilot whale drive. I say I would rather live in a world where no one kills a whale or a dolphin. But they rarely share my special affection for cetaceans.

In Faroes, the very act of killing is part of a pattern of life and death that has been unchanged for a millennium. Small children watch animals being killed – the business of slaughter is ingrained in the rhythm of life. A friend recently told me that he was irritated that his father-in-law had taken his four-year-old son to watch a bull being killed at a neighbour's farm. 'Because the child might have had nightmares after seeing the slaughter?' I ventured. 'No,' he said, 'because it was almost eleven o'clock at night and my son should have been in bed at nine.'

Perhaps killing is neither good nor bad. On a sliding scale, the slaughter of a marine mammal seems much less immoral and damaging to the planet than cutting down trees in the tropics to free up land to grow cattle feed so that obese people can eat hamburgers. Furthermore, pilot whale meat isn't wrapped in plastic when it travels from the sea to the Faroese table. After a whale drive, all of the organic waste, the bones and vestigial flesh from the carcases, is returned to the deep sea. But behind all the intellectual arguments, and above and beyond the ethics of slaughtering animals, the *grind* presents me with a deeply personal challenge. I couldn't predict how it would feel to help kill a whale. It might bring lifelong guilt, or I might feel nothing. It was possible I might experience an atavistic thrill. I had the power to say yes or no, but if I did it then it would involve confronting personal demons, and perhaps lead to a recognition that there was something primitive at my core. I know that if I took part in killing a pilot whale, I would be allowing the possibility of death, of nothingness and nihilism into my heart. There would be nothing sacred left in the world, and the eight-year-old boy who cried when he killed a toad would be gone for ever.

* * *

The day after the recent *grind*, I go to Jóhannus's house as he prepares his share of the meat. In his small basement, the place where he slaughters and butchers his sheep, I watch him separate the large square chunks of flesh and blubber into log-shaped strips as wide as my thigh and longer than my forearm. The richly sheened meat shows scarcely any lines of fat beneath the surface, just a paper-thin layer where it was joined to the thick outer blubber. Larger pieces of dirty white blubber lie on the basement floor like safety mats in a gym. Neat segments of blubber are carefully stacked on top of one another, lined up verti-cally around the inside of a large tub like the bricks of an igloo and covered with a thick layer of salt. They will stay there for several months. The fresh red meat is in chunks, bigger than any piece of animal flesh I have ever seen. Each weighs four or five kilograms, and Jóhannus slices them with a fifteen-centimetre blade, a hunting knife sharp as a razor. He eyes each strip like a diamond cutter judging a stone, looking for the best place to carve into it and make meal-sized joints. 'I aim for about two or three kilograms apiece,' he says, 'and that will make dinner for four or five people. It will shrink a little as it cooks.'

Pilot whale meat tastes like good-quality beef, and has little fat. As you chew it, the consistency breaks down, a little like well-cooked liver. If well rinsed and prepared properly, it does not have an oily or fish-like taste. Jóhannus wants longer, thinner slabs of muscle for making sausage. He rolls the strips and squeezes them into a mesh sleeve so that they can be hung to dry in the *hjallur* behind his parents' house for several months to harden and gain their bloom. 'If we eat it fresh then we must soak it in water and vinegar overnight. That will take away any fishy taste from the meat,' Jóhannus explains. 'It needs to be boiled for five or six hours and then roasted in the oven for another two hours.'

I watch him stroke the slabs of wine-dark meat with his fingers, feeling the grain and assessing the best fillets to save as steaks. He lets me cut some slices, watching carefully that I make long, confident strokes into the meat. 'You must make a single straight cut – no sawing – we don't want any slits or holes in the meat when it's hanging,' he warns. 'That is where a fly could get in and lay its eggs.' The newly sharpened blade makes swift work of this solid flesh which has been soaking in running water and is cold to the touch. It is hefty, clean and sensuously smooth. My hands smell of fresh steak, and the scent in the air is rich and primal. At times like this, I envy Jóhannus his practical view of the world, and the animals within it.

Ravens VII

Mid June

Once there were white ravens in Faroes. In Iceland and Greenland, there were occasional etiolated versions of these famously black birds, but only in Faroes were they seen regularly and in significant numbers. The *hvitravnur* occurs in folk songs from the fifteenth century, when they were said to be very common. Nineteenth-century ornithologists twice declared them a separate sub-species, naming them *Corvus leucophaeus*, and *Corvus variegates færøensis*. They are now known to be a simple colour mutation of Faroes' northern raven, *Corvus corax varius*. The Faroese anomaly was consistent in appearance, with a white head and solid-black back, and white primary and secondary flight feathers. They were not albinos, but genuine colour mutations caused by a recessive gene being passed on by both parents. It's a type of colour variant called 'leucism' and it differs from 'albinism' because the bird is not totally missing melanin, and has normal, or just slightly paler-coloured eyes.

Faroese ravens today are uniformly black, possibly less glossy than their counterparts in the rest of Europe. In the early eighteenth century, a Danish visitor described 'large flocks of speckled ravens'. In his broad account of life in Faroes in 1673,

Lucas Debes wrote that he had kept a white raven as a pet, and 'in a notable experiment' trained it to call his house boy Erasmus. Eventually, the boy killed the bird, 'for the mischief it did'. It was, of course, human mischief that exterminated the famous white ravens, as they were sought after as museum specimens and fetched a high price among collectors. More than two dozen are displayed in museums around the world as far afield as Vienna, Paris, New York, Edinburgh, Uppsala and, naturally, Copenhagen. There is also a rather handsome specimen in the British Natural History Museum collection at Tring in Hertfordshire. This bird, mounted on a branch, even has a pale beak with matching feet, as well as a rather dashing white cap of head feathers. There have been similar ravens spotted in Canada in recent years, and the gene may still be present in Faroes, so it's just possible that a speckled raven could reappear one day.

The pure-white-headed fulmars, some of them at least, are now guarding their single eggs. They remain more interested in squabbling with one another than in anything else. I have been watching one bird which keeps settling itself comfortably on its grassy seat beside an egg, rather than on top of it. I wonder if the neglected egg is a failed effort by another fulmar, and if the mother has her own egg safely brooding, but the ground is too uneven to get a clear view.

I rarely find the adult ravens in the gorge now, but I see them high over the fjord quite some distance from the nest. They always head determinedly southwards, never flying north towards the road and the empty sheep pen. I get the impression the chicks are being kept low on food, perhaps to encourage them to think about leaving the nest. They have started to venture out more often, stepping gingerly around the small steep area of grass inside the nook. One chick is bolder than the others, and I nervously watch it teetering and sliding on the sloping ground. It investigates clumps of moss and some straggly ferns with its beak, pulling at the greenery in vain. There is nothing edible there. It spies a bone deep in the outer wall of the nest and ferrets between the desiccated twigs to pluck it out. It's a tiny fragment, perhaps from a dead hare, but utterly dried out and ancient-looking with no trace of meat on it at all. I can see other bones, even a tiny lamb scapula among the jack-straws pile that has supported the chicks since birth. The boldest raven spends almost half an hour investigating every corner of the tiny rock niche, and then climbs back up to the nest. Watchful shapes, the other two birds stand shoulder to shoulder on the rim, hunch-backed and glowering at their adventurous sibling.

Leaving the ravens is getting harder. I am convinced they must be near to fledging. I want them to fly, but I don't know how easy it will be for them to leave the nest safely. Below the nook, the water is unrippled, shadowed and still. Black as oil.

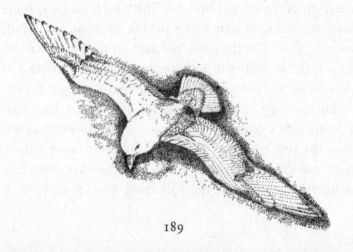

8

Sea Horse Eggs

Sandoy, June

I have a memory of a solitary fulmar flying up a vertical basalt wall above a leaden ocean. The breast and head of the bird are the same pale shade as the narrow strip of visible sky, but the trailing edge of the wings is the colour of cigarette smoke, matching the low clouds that shroud the top of the cliffs. It moves like a swift gust of wind, silently with barely a flicker of movement in its wide wings, their plumage blending with grey rain and rock. The moisture in the air is so fine I feel it, atomised, entering my lungs as I breathe. This bird lives long, some say sixty years, in that moist tumult of stone and wind, water and air. On the cliffs, perched on their bare narrow ledges, the brooding time is just a momentary stillness in decades of incessant motion on and above a frigid ocean.

Fulmar eggs make good eating if they are less than a week old. Collecting the eggs means climbing down onto the tiny rock perches where the birds make a basic nest, usually high above the sea. On Sandoy, the cliffs at Lonin have been an egg-collecting spot for more than a century. Benjámin Lydersen, who lent me his hat on Mykines, invites me to go to the island. His family come from Sandoy, and he knows the men who will go to the cliffs to collect eggs, weather permitting.

Benjámin meets me off the ferry at Skopun on the north coast, and drives me across the island to where we will start the walk to the bird cliffs of Lonin. They lie on the west coast of Sandoy, not far from Søltuvík bay, the spot where the *Principia* ran aground in 1895. We make a brief stop at the shoreline to see the two great anchors retrieved from the wreck and the small stone monument to the men who lost their lives on board. The sea is benign today and there are seals resting on the rocks at the southern edge of the bay. Benjámin says that this was a popular spot for collecting seaweed after a storm to use as fertiliser on the farms.

Sandoy is one of the lower-lying islands, the highpoint less than 500 metres above the Atlantic. Benjámin drives along the narrow winding roads, pointing out landmarks he has known all his life. There is something fluttering in the distance, something caught in a sheep fence by the side of the road, and I ask him to stop. As we get out of the car, there is the rank stench of decay and I can see that it is not one thing, but two dead birds side by side, a hooded crow and a seagull. They have been tied with string to the wire. Benjámin stretches the wing of the gull out for me to examine, saying it's something he doesn't see very often. He says it's to scare away birds from the domestic geese and their goslings. The feathers move gently in the breeze and the sickly sweet smell of rot wafts over us. The birds are pinned there like voodoo charms, and I find it disturbing.

Benjámin is easy company and in a cheerful mood, pleased to show me his island. He says we will walk for an hour or more to reach the bird cliffs, and parks the car on a muddy farm track just off the coastal road. We set off north on a steady climb and just as we crest the first ridge, I see a straggling line of figures spread out across the open moor. We catch them up, and Benjámin makes introductions. They are all from Sandoy, and I recognise Hallur, one of the local helicopter pilots who has flown me between the islands on several occasions. We talk about flying and the challenges of Faroes weather.

We cross a wide stretch of moorland where a substantial stream provides a welcome place for everyone to get a drink. It's one of those days when walking across the undulating open ground allows you to believe it is really quite warm, but a few minutes standing around talking and drinking the chilled water from the beck is a reminder that in Faroes heat is a relative term. During the pause, I am introduced to Bjarki Henriksen, a tall wiry man who seems to be in charge. He wants to know which islands I have been to in Faroes, and how much I know about collecting bird eggs. He is reassured when I say I met Benjámin catching gannets, and that I have had fulmar eggs before. He carries a hard hat, a length of rope and a bag festooned with karabiners that jangle as he walks. He tells me he is fifty-nine, and that he went to sea at the age of fifteen. As we walk, he pauses suddenly, spotting something and veering off to show me a hollow in the ground where there is a curlew's nest – four richly speckled eggs, one of the first clutches of the season, on a thin bed of dry grass. Dull olive green, they are patterned as if lightly drizzled with melted chocolate.

We continue walking and climb a steep bank to reach another open expanse of moorland, which slopes gently to the west. Ahead there is a small brightly painted green hut all alone on the open ground about a hundred metres from the cliff edge. Inside there are two young men drinking coffee, one of them Bjarki's son David, who is twenty-three. The hut smells strongly of diesel, and half of the internal space is taken up with a large engine. A fan belt drives a drum which is wound thickly around with rope. There is a small table and a couple of rickety hard-back chairs. Coils of climbing rope, anoraks and water-proof trousers hang in a dense forest on the back wall and the table is littered with cartons of milk, tea and coffee, assorted packets of biscuits and a bowl of miniature choc-olate bars. There are flasks of hot water and I am invited to take whatever I want.

Stepping outside to escape the fuel smell inside, I see that there is an opening in the front wall of the cabin, like a badger-sized cat-flap, and from it emerges a rope that snakes along the ground to the cliff edge. A few wooden contraptions are spaced every twenty metres along the ground, crude guide tracks fitted with a grooved plastic wheel over which the rope runs. Benjámin is in charge of making sure the rope stays on its guide path. At the cliff edge, the rope passes over an iron bar jammed into the rocks, like the top rung of a ladder. There is a small cleft in the granite here, a natural opening just wide enough for a man to clamber down. I crawl to the edge and peer over to find a sickening vertical drop 300 metres to the water below.

There is much chatter, and more tea and coffee, and Hallur seems to have taken charge of the diesel engine. He perches on a high seat operating a handle that stops and starts the drum, controlling the speed of the rope as it spools out. Bjarki emerges from the hut with his hard hat and his gloves on. Tied to his side is a container, a plastic jerry can with the spout sawn off. At the cliff edge, he bends down, tears off some clumps of grass and stuffs them into the bottom of the container where he will place any eggs he finds on the cliffs. From the hut he has also brought a bamboo pole, perhaps a metre and a half long. At one end there is a metal ring holding a string net no bigger than the pocket on a billiard table. The diesel engine is coughing and spluttering in the background and smoke signals belch from a thin exhaust pipe on the side of the green hut.

Bjarki gathers his equipment and attaches himself to a safety line with his karabiners. Hans Jacob, a younger man with a luxuriant beard, stations himself right at the cliff edge, harnessed to a line which is tied in turn to a wooden stake about a metre high buried deep in the ground. He is there, he explains, to watch that the climber below is OK, and keep an eye on the rope to make sure it moves freely over the lip of the cliff. I watch as Bjarki walks backwards over the cliff edge and gives a cheerful wave as he disappears from view. He does it without fuss or ceremony. It is impossible to see him once he descends, as there is a small overhang just a couple of metres below the iron bar. The rope moves along its runners and Hans Jacob sits on his precarious look-out post communicating by walkie-talkie with Hallur about the speed of the rope being let out from the hut.

I walk along the coast a little way and have views north and west to where the Trøllhøvdi pokes out from the tip of Sandoy. My eye traces an arc of land masses, the west coast of Koltur, the south coast of Vágar and finally the green bump of Mykines to the west. There are birds on the faces of the walls and sea stacks below me, and white shapes soaring away and towards the cliffs. Many will be fulmars but some are kittiwakes, impossible to tell apart from up here.

Bjarki has been down on the cliff face for more than half an hour when a shout goes up and I see the thick rope begin to travel backwards along the ground and through the 'cat-flap' in the green hut. Benjámin trots up and down its length, making sure it doesn't snag or escape from the wooden runners. After a few minutes, I spot Bjarki's climbing helmet poking up above the cliff edge, and then he scrambles over the iron bar and onto the grass. He is all smiles as he begins to unclip himself from the rope. He carefully hands the plastic container slung around his neck to Benjámin, and everyone troops back to the hut. Outside it, we gather around as the eggs are unwrapped like precious treasures from their grassy cocoon. Bjarki has more than a dozen, and he arranges them in neat rows on the ground.

Behind the hut, there is a large cooking pot filled with water being heated by a primus stove, which hisses loudly. 'We will try some!' Bjarki says triumphantly. Fresh tea and coffee are made and handed around while the eggs are cooking. It takes twenty minutes and we stand in the sun ready for the first taste of this seasonal treat. Eventually, Benjámin hands me an egg and I weigh it in my hand it's closer in size to a duck's egg than a chicken's. I pick the shell off carefully and find the white undamaged. It shines like fine alabaster, translucent and flawless, and at its centre there is sunburst yellow. It tastes deliciously light and fluffy, rich and fresh. The yolk tastes the same as a hard-boiled hen's egg, but the white is more delicate, somehow less rubbery and more subtle in flavour, and surprisingly, given the fulmar's diet, with no hint of fishiness. Everyone is very pleased, and now there are others ready to take their turn on the cliffs.

* * *

Vágar, late August

It's nine in the evening but the sun is still a dazzling orange ball above the horizon. At the entrance to the fjord between Vágar and Streymoy, the tide is strong. Vilhelm Hansen steers the small single-engined motor cruiser *Emma* expertly through the narrows and heads for the open ocean. Mysterious eddies and bright foaming white horses swirl together close to the point marked on the chart as Slættanestangi. The currents can reach eight knots here, and even with a modern boat it pays to keep a close eye on the tide race. The air is fresh, and the tang of salt invigorating. The distant glowing orb is like a magnet pulling us towards the edge of the world.

The water deepens underneath us, somehow more opaque and potent as we leave the fjord, hiding unseen sleeping things carried from the eternal depths. There is land out there if you go far enough on a north-west heading. Four hundred and fifty kilometres away, you'd hit Iceland, not an option in this little boat. The ninety-horse-power engine buzzes like an angry wasp, shrieking as the cruiser bucks and rolls leaving the shelter of the sound. Vilhelm is Jóhannus's older brother, and like many Faroese men he worked on fishing boats in challenging conditions catching shrimp, cod and haddock off Greenland and Norway for several years before coming home to have a family. He is dark-haired, lean and strong with the physique of a footballer, and more serious than his younger sibling. Vilhelm knows everything about boats and engines and if, St Brendan-like, he said we *were* sailing to Iceland, I would trust him to get us there.

At the stern, Jóhannus is busy assembling the tools he needs for this expedition to catch fulmar chicks. The young birds jump and glide down from their high perches on the cliffs, chubby and round-chested after being fed for about seven weeks by both parents. The fledglings will float offshore for several days after leaving their clifftop nests for the first time, too fat to fly and waiting to lose weight. The current takes them further and further offshore in that time, which is why they must be caught soon after they jump.

Jóhannus is now surrounded by hunting paraphernalia: cable ties and an upturned milk crate, some plastic sheeting to cover the seats of the boat and a net at the end of a long pole. There's a stiff wind, and all three of us are wearing oilskins and woollen hats. 'Wind is good,' Vilhelm observes. 'The birds need a bit of breeze to jump from the cliffs the first time. These are the right conditions, but it's maybe too early, I haven't heard of anyone catching any chicks yet in this area.'

The cliffs to our left are forbidding, in places over 500 metres high, and there is no visible human imprint on the land. This northern edge of Vágar is uninhabited now, though there were once two villages on this stretch of coast: Slættanes, empty since 1965, and further west in the next deep bay, Víkar, abandoned more than a century ago. The fulmars nest all along here, the more mature experienced birds taking the spots on the folded flanks of the topmost chimney crags. Jóhannus has taken me up to the precipitous ridge from the other side so that we could look down onto Víkar and watch the birds wheeling onto their high nests.

Tonight, it seems at first as if the sea is empty. Gradually, as I accustom my eyes to the glare and the contrasting shadows of the surface ripple, I notice that there are little black birds, floating here and there. They are puffins, which submerge if we approach too close with the boat, or take off with a splashing fluttering commotion.

Vilhelm and Jóhannus stand with legs akimbo and braced against the swell, scanning the water for any sign of birds. It's not easy against the glaring sunset which has turned the water into a dark carpet that flows to infinity. Then, without a word of warning, Vilhelm swings the wheel violently to the right and guns the throttle. He has seen a chick several hundred metres away. Jóhannus quickly takes up position on the bench seat at the rear of the little open cabin and readies the net. We pass within a metre of the bird which bobs calmly on the surface and disappears inside the net without a sound. Jóhannus deftly swings it inboard and with one hand pulls the fulmar smoothly and gently from the mesh. Without pause, he grips the bird behind the wings in his left hand. Dropping the net handle across his lap, he bends its head backwards and with two fingers of his other hand around its neck stretches it downwards. The fulmar goes limp, and he squeezes its plump stomach. A stream of orange liquid cascades out of its open beak onto the water and he shakes it briskly to get the last drops away before slipping a cable tie around its neck (to contain any further stomach oil) and placing the corpse head down into one of the slots in the crate. 'I leave them there for a few minutes so that they cool down,' Jóhannus explains. 'If I pile the birds up together in the box when they are warm it's not good for the meat.' And so it goes. Vilhelm spots the birds and gives chase. Jóhannus catches them, despatches them and stores them in the bottle crate. When all the slots are full, he takes out the birds that have been in the crate longest and places them in neat rows inside a cooler box on the floor of the boat. He works quickly and efficiently.

The chattering and barracking of the adult fulmars has

been a constant accompaniment to my time at the ravens' nest. I have watched them soar in from the sea on their stiff wings, controlling their position with barely a flick of the tail.

In the first written description of these birds in 1603, they were called *haffhest* – Norse for 'sea horse', and in Faroes today they are *havhestur*. The English term fulmar is less attractive, and seems to have come from another Norse phrase, 'foul-gull', a clear reference to their habit of projectile vomiting a stream of extremely viscous stomach oil at assailants or other species that come too close. They are not gulls at all, but members of the petrel family, and technically *Procellariiformes*, a group that includes the great oceanic wanderers like albatrosses, petrels and shearwaters. They all share the unusual feature of a tube on their upper bill, which encloses their nostrils. This adaptation seems to confer an enhanced sense of smell, and also serves to disperse salty snot from the body after drinking seawater.

The noxious-smelling oil, which is not just fishy but has a pungent, musty oldness about it, is partly a product of the tiny crustaceans and small fish the birds consume at sea. It varies in colour from virulent rapeseed yellow to blood red, although most commonly it has a urine-like tinge. If the oil hits another bird, such as a puffin, it effectively kills it by making its feathers clump together and matt, leaving it vulnerable to the cold, and also unable to fly. Fulmars have, it's said, even killed baby rabbits with their vomit. It's produced in a part of the bird's stomach called the proventriculus, a sac at the bottom of the oesophagus just below the gizzard. In fulmars, the proventriculus is very baggy, and has thick wrinkled walls lined with glands that excrete the waxy oil which courting birds pass to one another in small amounts, perhaps as a way of scent-marking their mate. A bird normally has enough vomit to spray three times at an intruder or an enemy, and the liquid will easily travel two metres. The oil is extremely rich in vitamins A and D, and seems to be a way of storing nutrition for a week or longer, a useful trait for a bird that travels long distances across the ocean in search of food.

In Carolus Clusius's compendium of natural history *Exoticorum libri decem* (1605), he described the fulmar as a bird that made Faroese fishermen 'horribly afraid', as it was believed to be a portent of bad weather. At that time, the fulmars were generally only found further to the west, in Iceland, and so if they appeared near Faroes it was a sign of an approaching storm. The first recorded fulmar nests – on the southernmost island of Suðuroy –were not seen until early in the nineteenth century. They gradually spread north and east, and by 1900 they were nesting all over the islands, so successfully colonising the cliffs that within thirty years the Faroese were collecting as many as 80,000 chicks in one week in autumn. A similar pattern occurred in the British Isles, with the birds appearing in St Kilda around the same time they reached Faroes. On St Kilda, fulmars eventually displaced gannets and puffins as the staple food, with each islander eating more than 120 birds a year. For the St Kildans, the bird also provided oil for their lamps and feathers which they used to pay their annual rent. The local people were so isolated that when outsiders visited they often brought with them infections to which the islanders had no resistance, and which they always called a 'boat cough'. The preferred remedy was, in the words of one visitor, 'the fat of their fowls, with which they stuff the stomach of a gannet, in the fashion of a pudding. This they put in an infusion of oatmeal, which in their language they call Brochan.'

In the late nineteenth century, St Kilda was afflicted by a terrible spate of infant mortality, with over eighty per cent of babies dying within eight days of birth. The visiting doctor blamed the fulmars, as he observed the local midwife smearing umbilical cords with oil from the birds (stored in a gannet stomach) as an antiseptic. Only recently has it been found that the babies were succumbing to infant tetanus, which came from contaminated soil on the island, and not the fulmars.

Years ago in Faroes, I met a man on a sailing boat who told me he loved to catch fulmars and eat them. 'But I won't be doing it this year,' he lamented. 'Because my girlfriend is pregnant and they carry a disease that is very dangerous for babies and expectant mothers.'

He wasn't talking about the phantom bacteria of St Kilda, but a genuine risk of psittacosis, a type of pneumonia sometimes called 'parrot fever'. It comes from *Chlamydophila psittaci*, a bacterium which infects as many as ten per cent of fulmar chicks. Fulmars across the Atlantic were the source of an outbreak of psittacosis in the 1930s, one so virulent that in Faroes handling the birds was totally forbidden until 1954. Between 1933 and

1937, Faroes had 165 cases, almost twenty per cent of which were fatal. The disease always struck in September, the time when people were handling and plucking fulmar carcases. The fulmar expert James Fisher, discovered some years later that it was highly probable that the fulmars of Faroes had contracted the disease from pecking at the corpses of Amazonian parrots thrown overboard in their thousands after an outbreak of the disease on board ships transporting them from Brazil to Europe for sale as exotic pets. There have been sporadic cases of psittacosis since then, but none have been fatal, as the disease is easily cured with antibiotics.

* * *

After an hour or so on the water, Jóhannus has caught almost fifty birds. Vilhelm is nearly always the first to spot them, try as I might to find one before him. Occasionally we approach a bird and it flies away, proof that it is an adult fulmar. The chicks rarely escape, although some manage to flutter a few metres out of reach until they tire and end up in the net. Jóhannus asks if I want to try catching, and we swap places so that I can sit in the stern with the net.

It's easy enough to scoop the young fulmars up, thanks to Vilhelm's skill at sweeping within a metre or two of them with the boat. An early nature writer described fulmars as having a 'cold Arctic eye', but it doesn't seem that way to me. Their eyes are bright, beady and full of life and energy. The birds are warm to the touch and extremely soft. As I reach into the net, they open their beaks wide and spew their stomach oil. Sometimes they manage to peck me, though it's nothing to be afraid of. The trick is to keep them at arm's length for the first few moments and not bring them inside the boat until they have finished vomiting. Inevitably I get oil on my catching hand, and the side of the boat is splattered. I am struck again by the pristine whiteness of the fulmar's head feathers, and how plump these chicks are on their first and only excursion from the nest. Mostly, the deed is done smoothly, and without gore. In the moment of execution there is no high drama. I grasp the bird firmly but gently behind the wings with my left hand and grip the back of its head in my right. With my first two fingers either side of the skull I tip the head back and then pull firmly in a straight line with a downward pressure. I can feel the neck stretch for a split second as the cervical spine detaches like pulled elastic. As the bird hangs limply upside down, I squeeze its stomach so as to release any remaining oil into the water. They are not hard to kill, although I am anxious not to have a maimed or paralysed bird on my conscience, and sometimes stretch the neck too violently so that the head comes off and a thin fountain of blood shoots up. Jóhannus is unimpressed.

Ravens VIII

Mid June

A large colony of Arctic terns has gathered on the coast not far from the gorge. They are delicate creatures, identical in shape to the fairy terns I know so well from the Indian Ocean, and, like them, they lay a single egg on the ground, without a nest. The tropical birds will also lay their tiny egg on a branch, balancing it precariously in a hollow in the bark. These northern birds don't have the luxury of trees, but they are just as dainty-looking. But, instead of being totally white, they have a smart black cap that covers the top of the head from the base of the beak to the nape of the neck, extending just below the eye, like a mediæval executioner's mask. Their bodies have a slight blue-grey tint that reminds me of old-fashioned airmail writing paper, and their deeply forked tails are so porcelain white that they glow translucent even against this northern sky. They rise up as a fluttering cloud at my approach, showing their rouged feet and beaks, shrieking with their oh-so-rapid crying, *kjeee-ooh-kjeee-ooh-kjeee-ooh-tchuk-tchuk-tchuk-tchuk*. The noise is hard to tolerate for long; in fact, there is a Faroese word – *ternudimmi* – meaning literally 'just for a moment', denoting the briefest of times in the summer night when the terns fall blessedly silent. But perhaps they deserve their socialising time, since they fly further in a lifetime than any other bird – and probably make the longest migration of any animal on earth, back and forth between the Arctic and the Antarctic, up to 100,000 kilometres a year. They fly in search of endless summer, with individual birds only nesting once every three years.

I am glad to find the peace of the ravens' hideaway. A pair of shags is fishing just offshore. Unlike the glossy untarnished ravens, the shags seem scruffy and look like they work hard to feed their scrawny frames. The wind ruffles the little feather crest above their eyes, and the plainness of their silhouettes against the water is relieved by their bright yellow underbills which catch the sun as they surface from a dive. Almost always, small fish glisten in their mouths when they reappear, and with one all-over quiver the birds immediately shed every bead of moisture from their feathers.

I am on the promontory, watching the rock ledges where the kelp swirls at the entrance to the gorge. A female eider comes in low and fast, feet splayed and wings held high, crashing clumsily into the water. She bobs around where the seaweed grows thickly, and near to where the big waterfall enters the sound. The tide is running hard and fighting against an easterly wind, producing a slight surface chop, and it's some time before I notice that there are more than twenty black guillemots within a hundred metres of where I am sitting. Only with my binoculars can I see that there are many more specks of life out in mid-channel.

To get out of the chilling wind, I climb the slope to my usual perch, and after just a few minutes, I hear a sharp *krork-krork*. The old Faroese name for raven is *gorpur*, and must surely be onomatopoeic. Raising my head cautiously, I spot an adult raven. It has landed on the almost vertical cliff wall and is clinging to a small tuft of grass about ten metres from the nest. It calls again, three or four times, a low throaty *gruk-grark-gruk-grark*. The chicks all turn in the direction of the sound, though they cannot see the adult bird from inside their niche in the rockface. After just a few seconds, the adult takes off again, flying up the cleft and past the nest calling twice, but now with a more shrill *gark-guy gark-guy* as it leaves. There is no food in its beak, and I believe it's trying to encourage the chicks to leave their pile of sticks and bones.

Later, two raven chicks totter out of the nest on foot. I watch them make the short hoppity journey down the sloping moss. They potter around the small steep ledge, pecking at the grass and pulling at strands of moss. Every time they pluck a strand of foliage they pause, looking around and up and down with quick twitches of the head. It's as if they are checking that no one is watching.

9

King of the Gannets

Swift white arrows soar above a granite sea on stiffened wings, necks outstretched and wide-set eyes fixed straight ahead. Nearer to land, free of the dark backdrop of water, I see that the birds are not pure white, but have dark wing tips, so neatly defined they could have been dipped in ink. Closer still, I can make out the caps of mustard yellow that cover their graceful heads down to the nape. It looks as if they have been freshly dusted with summer pollen. Those piercing hunters' eyes are ringed with palest cornflower blue, wistful pools of light set behind a strong tapering beak with a base thicker than my thumb. Gannets, here called *súla*, are goose-big, the largest birds in all of the North Atlantic, skimming the waves on wingspans as wide as a man is tall, plunging through the sea to collect fish and squid, anything they can catch with their stabbing beaks. Their streamlined bodies are padded with air sacks beneath the skin allowing them to hit the water at sixty miles an hour. As they dive they leave a champagne bubble trail that fizzes for a second or two after they disappear underwater. They return to Mykines, the most westerly island, each January, to court a mate. Tradition has it that they come to the island on the 25th, *Pálsmessu* – the Feast of the Conversion of St Paul. Once, the women of the village would run to the cliffs and wave their aprons in greeting to the gannets, welcoming them back to their nesting sites with a traditional dance.

Some of these wanderers have spent a few months wintering in Sicily and Sardinia, in the Mediterranean, but others have travelled over 6000 kilometres, from as far south as the coast of West Africa and the rich fishing grounds of Senegal and Mauritania. A few have even been right down in the Gulf of Guinea. It is the youngest birds which fly furthest, usually leaving Faroes in late September, while the fully mature adults will stay into November. Each summer, the birds grow whiter, moving from finely speckled grey to blotchy white and black, until they reach adult colouring at four or five years old.

On Mykines, nesting adults and surviving adolescent birds return to their nesting sites on the sheer cliff face on the northern side of Mykineshólmur. Forty metres above the sea, there are narrow rocky ledges where the birds build messy nests a foot or so apart, just enough distance to stop the chicks pecking each other as they grow. The gannets live on the fringes of this rocky place, and although records of the colony go back to 1500 and earlier, they nest nowhere else in Faroes. Some of the birds make their home on the nearby sea stacks of Píkarsdrangur and Flatidrangur, or on Bølið, a crumbling promontory barely attached to the islet at its most south-westerly edge. Aside from the sea stacks, the bulk of the colony of around two and a half thousand nesting pairs will roost on the narrow slimy ledges on the northern edge of the *hólm*, below the grassy sloping clifftop made green and lush by guano deposited by colonies of nesting puffins, gulls and petrels. The ledges down below have all been named too; Norðastarók, Urðin and Loftsrók, places slick with droppings and regurgitated fish. Here, the gannet pairs raise just one chick covered in wispy white down. Gradually, the fluff darkens as the first feathers appear, and by the time it is ready to launch itself into the sea below the rocks, the young gannet is elegantly flecked in a bespoke suit of black and grey. Before that it is a folded thing, all wing bones and disproportionately big webbed feet, gawky and adolescent with an oversized beak as its defence against the world. The chicks peer out into the Atlantic wind from a noisome pile of twigs, bones and feathers, waiting for a parent to return from foraging up to 200 kilometres offshore with another liquefied meal of herring or mackerel.

Mykineshólmur is the scene of an ornithological mystery. In 1894, it was recorded that an albatross had been shot on the cliffs where the gannets lived. Not only was this the most northerly sighting of the species at the time, but it was widely known on the island that this 'big gannet' had been living with the colony for over thirty years. The bird arrived each year with the gannets and had been spotted for thirty-four consecutive summers. It was so distinctive, because of its size, that the people of Mykines called it *Súlukongurin* ('King Gannet'). It was eventually shot by a local man, Johannes Frederik Joensen, apparently by accident when he fired at the cliffs to see if the bird would fly. No one on Mykines knew that the bird was an albatross, and assumed it was simply an unusually large gannet. The Victorian author Elizabeth Taylor said that Johannes Joensen had been one of her guides, and that his nickname had become 'Johannes of the Albatross'. A later examination of the bird's carcase in Denmark revealed that 'King Gannet' was actually a 'queen'.

They say that gannets came to the island as a gift. Like so many northern fables, the story concerns a giant pitted against a man. The giant, Tórur, lived at Gásadalur on nearby Vágar. Deciding that he wanted to own Mykines, the home of Óli the Mighty, Tórur jumped across the sea, creating the depression in the land that is the deep valley of Borgardalur at the eastern end of the island. Óli retreated west, calling out for a chasm to be created in the land separating the far end of the island from its bulk. Straddling the gap, Tórur began fighting Óli with his sword, but Óli managed to blind his attacker in one eye, and gradually start to win the battle. Tórur then offered Óli three gifts if he would only let him live. The first gift was that each year a large bottlenose whale would swim close to the island and be landed at Hvalagjógv. The second gift was that driftwood would wash up in the gorge known as Viðarhellisgjógv. Thirdly, Tórur promised that a bird would arrive on Mykineshólmur, and nest nowhere else in all of Faroes. These gifts would last so long as no one on the island ever spoke badly about any of them. According to the story, the whale duly arrived and was killed and eaten, and then criticised – either, as one version has it – because it only had one eye, or because after eating its flesh the Mykines residents fell ill. The driftwood too arrived, but people complained that it was knotted and twisted and unfit for lasting repairs on the village church. These gifts disappeared, but the gannets were always spoken of kindly and respectfully and remain nesting until now, only leaving the cliffs (tradition says) on St Martin's Day, 11th November.

Gannets have been recorded here since the sixteenth century, and in 1544 the English naturalist William Turner described the species as the 'Solend guse, a bird of the wandering un-settled sort, from whose fat the Scots make an ointment of great value in the treatment of many diseases'. Turner also noted that on Bass Rock in the Firth of Forth 'it tends its young with such affection that when boys are let down the face of the rock by means of ropes, for the purpose of carrying them off, it attacks them with great ferocity'. He added that the arrival of the birds on the Scottish east coast was a sign that the herring season had begun.

Some gannets are still taken and eaten in the Hebrides, from the uninhabited isle of Sula Sgeir forty miles north of Lewis, a tradition kept alive by a few men setting out once a year from the Port of Ness. And, just as they were in Scotland, the gannets of Mykines have been long valued as food. The Faroese gannet exerts a similar power on the local imagination. On Mykines, the traditional hunt is alive, kept going even though too few people live on the island to make it possible without extra help.

Jóhannus Hansen is one of the men who come to Mykines at this time of year to go down the cliffs. I joined him on the boat ride from the small port of Sørvágur to the island, one of thirty or so men in thickly knitted Faroese sweaters carrying rucksacks and supplies for the overnight expedition. Alongside his skills as a climber, and a mountain guide, above all he is a flagbearer for traditional subsistence types of husbandry. He adeptly juggles his modern life with the traditions he believes make Faroese culture special. He embodies the spirit of the *innløgumaður*, (pronounced *inny-loo-er-mer-vur*), a man who lives off the land.

From the island of Vágar it takes about forty minutes on the ferry to reach Mykines in good weather. On a map, Vágar looks uncannily like a dog's head in profile, looking west towards its smaller neighbour, complete with an upraised snout and open mouth. The lower jaw is separated from the upper by a long narrow inlet that ends at the little port of Sørvágur. Inland, the large freshwater lake Fjallavatn is in precisely the correct position to form the dog's 'eye'.

The boat to Mykines creeps out along the Sørvágsfjørður and then past the haunting shape of Tindhólmur, the craggiest islet in all of Faroes. It sits in line with the dog's open mouth – like a ball about to be caught – and is flanked in turn by the seastack of Drangarnir and then a small scone-shaped islet, Gáshólmur, which provides grazing for a few rams. Tindhólmur itself rises a fraction over 260 metres from the sea, soaring like a great green sail, with its southern side just a sheer rock wall. A castellated spine, ragged and foreboding, it is topped with five rock peaks, Ysti ('Farthest'), Arni ('Eagle'), Lítli ('Little'), Breiði ('Broad') and Boygdi ('Bent'). Tindhólmur is a symbol of these islands, dramatic and isolated, with an aura of mystery around those high gnarled pinnacles. On a foggy day there is a particular oddness to this rock, an otherworldliness suggesting it has been cleaved by a giant's axe. That vertical southern face makes it seem as thin and insubstantial as a movie-set façade; it's utterly bleak compared to the other side, which is covered by grass and moss all the way to the top. Seen from Vágar, the sharp silhouette of Tindhólmur easily resembles the crested outline of a sleeping sea-dragon. On the green northern side, there is a wide plateau just above sea level that appears to flow into the sea as a billowing basalt skirt. The blackened rock descends in a series of shelves towards the water, like eddies of cold hardened wax from a succession of candles that have oozed onto a dining table and solidified after a late-night dinner.

This island too has its fable. Jóhannus tells me that once an eagle stole a baby from a couple who farmed the flat slopes on the northern side of the peaks. Rasmus, the farmer, had been banished to the islet as punishment for a crime. Although his wife climbed the pinnacle and retrieved the baby from the bird's eyrie, the eagle had pecked out its eyes and the infant died. The distraught parents left the land and no one tried to live there again. Tindhólmur is still uninhabited, and privately owned by a few dozen individuals. Sheep are put out on the island, and they must be rounded up in autumn by men who make the boat trip from Vágar. A few rams are even left on the small areas of grazing on the craggy southern edge and to reach them the farmers must scale the spine, albeit at its lowest part, to cross over and collect them.

It seems like every valley in these islands has a story to tell. Looking back from the boat towards Vágar, I can see the shadowed bowl of Gásadalur surrounded by mountains on three sides. Gásadalur (Goose Valley) is famous for a waterfall that spurts from the cliffs below the village straight into the sea sixty metres below. It's common in high winds to see the water blowing back up the cliff face and billowing over the lip in great clouds of spray. It's a tiny place, and for centuries was extremely isolated. The settlement had no road access until 2004, and three times each week its postman had to walk over the 500-metre-high mountain from the village of Bøur to deliver the mail. It's a steep climb, and along the way there is a stone that marks the place where men from Gásadalur would pause for a rest when they had to carry a coffin from the village all the way to Bøur for burial. Jóhannus tells a story of how he first made the journey over the mountain alone when he was only six. While his grandfather Vilhelm watched his progress from the village through binoculars, his father waited and kept a lookout from the other side of the mountain. There is a photograph of Jóhannus in a blue tracksuit at the base of the steep path out of the valley with Rap, the family sheepdog for company. On the way up the track, he likes to relate how he met a family of Danish tourists who asked him to show them the way. Halfway up the mountain, they decided it was too steep a climb and gave up.

In one of the houses in Gásadalur there is a small wooden barrel that has been passed down through many generations by the descendants of a tenant farmer named Joen Johannesen and his wife Anna. Distant forebears of Jóhannus in the early nineteenth century, they farmed on king's land and had several daughters but no son to inherit the property and keep it going in their old age. The story goes that they were friendly with a French sea captain who came regularly to the island and that, at her husband's suggestion, Anna slept with him to try to get a son. The resulting baby, born in 1837, was christened Johannus Joensen but everyone called him 'Fransurin' ('the Frenchman'). He in turn called his own son Samuel Jacob 'Frants' Joensen. The little barrel was given to the farmer as a token of friendship by the sea captain.

* * *

With no tourists present, there is a party atmosphere on the ferry that afternoon when I first meet the gannet gang, men who all know each other, at least by sight. On the jetty at Mykines, it was Esbern, as usual, supervising disembarkation. His wife, Katrina, runs one of the few guesthouses on Mykines, and a café. Esbern is also the man who oversees the annual gannet catch, and is always first down the cliff to test the rope.

Up in the centre of the village, everyone goes into the small white-washed schoolhouse sitting square under its grass roof and signs their name on the *súlaveiða*, a register of whom exactly has helped with the gannet catch. There are no school-aged children on Mykines now, but the desks and chairs are there ready, in case they are needed. Oskar Joensen, whose washing machine I helped Esbern install, is supervising the unpacking of the very long rope stored in the schoolhouse loft. He is lean and outdoor-tanned with sapphire eyes that issue a gimlet gaze. The rope is the lifeline for the gannet catchers and will need to be carried out to Mykineshólmur, about an hour's hike from the village. Oskar is over eighty, and told me he had been a regular out on the cliffs until just two years earlier, and that he had spent much of his life as a merchant seaman. I watch him expertly tidy the thick rope and then arrange it neatly across an area of tarmac beside the school. Like so many Faroese seamen, he uses the old measurement, telling me it is 'sixty fathoms long' (112 metres).

In that bemusing timeless summer light, Jóhannus and eight other men assemble beside the white-washed building, taking up their places a few metres apart along the rope that Oskar has coiled at regular intervals marked with small pieces of knotted string or a strip of electrical tape. Each man has four coils of the thick rope in a sash across his shoulders for the journey out to the cliffs. In addition to the cumbersome rope, the men each have their own rucksack, and some have helmets and spare items of clothing as well as food and something to drink, on what would turn out to be a long night in the open. The rope party lead the procession of forty or so individuals out of the village and up the grass slope leading westward. The island narrows here, and the ridge extends west-south-west like a pot handle to the break in the land and the gorge where the sea rushes through the ocean channel between the two land masses. Leaving the village, the summer evening is dry, and the air still. At the crest of the ridge the procession pauses for a few minutes at the memorial for men from the island lost over the years at sea, or on the cliffs. The earliest name recorded is Anthonius Mortensen, who fell while fowling in 1757. Several of the men have told me that they enjoyed helping with the gannet hunt, but that going down the cliffs was definitely not for them. I was soon to discover why.

The rope party and the helpers carry on along the grass sheep track to the headland, eventually turning down a steep path leading through the puffin burrows to reach the bridge across the gorge. Descending the rocky steps to the bridge, we pass within a few feet of curious puffins and nesting kittiwakes. Once across the bridge, the path goes uphill again and onto a flatter grassy area where the ruins of a stone croft provide another rest stop. The light gradually dims from the sky and the men sit on the remnants of the old stone walls, chatting quietly while some of them bring out their food supplies. Away from the village, on this more exposed ground, a steady low wind blows from the south. The chattering sound of Leach's storm petrels comes from burrows in the grass, and from under some of the stones piled around the croft. A tall muscular man with close-cropped hair sitting alone on the wall offers me slices of *skerpikjøt* (fermented lamb) and traditional bread. We have never met, but he introduces himself as Benjámin, and tells me he is originally from Sandoy, before asking in a concerned voice if I have any 'warm clothes'. I am wearing an undershirt, a merino wool climbing jersey as well as a sweatshirt and then a Gore-tex anorak. He ferrets through his rucksack and produces a woollen hat and a pair of gloves. 'Take these,' he says, with a frown. To be polite, I accept the offer. It seems unnecessary when all around me many of the men are not wearing coats, only woollen sweaters.

Esbern sits among the ruins talking to Jens-Kjeld Jensen, the best-known ornithologist in the country, nick-named 'the bird man of Nólsoy'. After half an hour or so, Esbern gives the signal to start the last climb up the steeply angled slope to the cliff edge. Looking backwards and to the south, it is impossible to see exactly where the sky meets the sea. In the flat evening light, there are no shadows or reflections, and the two elements are united like a sheet of annealed steel. As we walk northwards up the sloping ground, the wind gains strength, and I realise that Benjámin's woollen hat is a far better idea than the flimsy hood on my coat, and jam it on over my ears. Even so, within half an hour I am cold, and on the cliff edge there is nothing, no hillock, no shrub, not even a grassy mound, to shield from the wind.

In the half-light, the men all know their roles. A few feet from the edge of the cliff there are stout wooden stakes buried in the soil, around which the rope can be wound while it is played out. One man is in charge of a thin safety line, and each gannet hunter about to descend the cliff is given a walkie-talkie as he steps into a wool-lined harness which encircles his thighs and buttocks for the journey downwards. Another concession to modernity are hard hats with head-torches affixed. As ever, each man has his hunting knife strapped to his belt. Jóhannus had asked me on the boat if I carried a knife and chanted the Faroese maxim: 'a man without a knife, is a man without a life' (*knívleysur maður er lívleysur maður*). I did not.

It is now impossible to see what becomes of the men as they step into the harness and disappear over the edge of the cliff. The high point of the ridge is almost 140 metres above the sea, but it seems a fathomless drop into infinite darkness. I join the line of men holding onto the rope, a giant one-sided tug-of-war team whose job it is to lower the line smoothly and at a manageable rate in the gloom. '*Lora!*' comes the command as the climbers go down, and '*Hiva!*' when they reach the ledge sixty metres below the lip of the cliff. Then, the harness has to be raised and readied for the next gannet catcher to descend. In the gloom, the men will shuffle carefully along the slippery cliff ledges to grab the chicks one at a time.

I quickly learn that taking a turn on the rope is the best way to stay warm. We are strung out along the length of it, up to twenty-five men moving up and down the top of Mykineshólmur. The surface of the islet is roughly rect-angular, like a dining table, but so steeply angled that it would have legs on one side a sixth the height of the other. When the empty harness is raised you have to move fast to keep up, trotting down the uneven ground, barely able to see where you are putting your feet. At the bottom of the slope, we stand catching our breath and waiting for the order to walk back upwards as the rope is played out over the cliff edge, but this time carrying the weight of the gannet catcher. Pulling the rope upwards with the man in harness requires a new command, '*Draga!*' (Pull!). A few of the men on the rope have head-torches, but mostly the work takes place in the dark. The other men are feature-less shapes at best, but there is comfort in their presence, in the sound of their breathing and in the soft glow here and there of a cigarette glowing in the distance. The wind blows steadily, and talking is difficult as we listen out for the shouted commands from the clifftop. This is serious work, and everyone knows that the life of the man on the cliff face depends on the rope being handled properly. I learn that the walkie-talkies are an innovation, brought in because a year earlier a gannet-catcher had put out his hand to steady his ascent and caught his fingers in a cleft in the cliff face. He shouted out for the rope team to stop pulling, but no one heard him and he left part of one finger trapped in the rocks.

The rope party move along the cliff edge, stopping when they reach a new lowering spot. Several men are sent down at each location (a few hundred metres apart), and left there during the darkest hours to catch the gannets. The birds are calmer then and easily dazzled by the men's torches. The hunters will be gone for several hours, choosing only the young birds which are just about to fledge. These are *grásúla,* grey gannets. Any chick with fluffy down still on its head will be spared. Birds caught too young, *ompil,* are not good to eat.

People begin hunkering down in the grass to doze, or to chat and eat their snacks. No one seems to have a mat or anything warm to keep off the chill from the ground.

I try without luck to find a spot out of the wind, feeling my way cautiously to the end of the cliffs where there is a small lighthouse. In the dim light this proves foolhardy, as it is hard to see fissures in the cliff edge and so I shuffle cautiously lower down to where the old lighthouse keeper's cottage stands. I have a small torch in my bag and as I negotiate the sloping ground the beam occasionally catches the glimmer of a pair of eyes in the grass. Sheep. The house is sealed up and provides no shelter. Somehow the wind seems to be blowing equally hard against all four sides of the building. It is inescapable. Eventually I return to the clifftop, twenty metres from the lip, and lie on the bare grass. I curl up in a ball and wedge my head behind my small rucksack, a tactic that gives only minimal shelter from the wind. In spite of the cold, I somehow doze off at about three thirty am, but it isn't long before someone shakes me by the shoulder; 'Wake up! We're moving now.' A figure I don't recognise shuffles away in the half-light of dawn and I follow, bleary-eyed and chilled to the bone, back towards the clifftop where the rope party is reassembling. It is time to bring the men up from below.

The rope gang pull in silence, listening carefully for the commands from the clifftop. Occasionally, the crackle of a walkie-talkie conversation carries through the air, and down to us on the lower slope. Pulling them up from below is more strenuous than lowering them down. The rope is as thick as my wrist with a heft to it that conveys great strength. Holding it feels like being part of a giant organic force, a tangible connection transmitting the combined physical strength of the team. There is a powerful rhythm to the work, a deep sense of masculine exertion that reminds me of the sensation of being in a top-class rowing eight. This gives the same feeling of working together in concert against an inert physical object – although this time the dead-weight is a man, rather than a boat. You know you are part of a force so much greater than whatever physical effort you can provide alone. The thread of the rope rubs against my palms, and I feel its course fibrous texture even through my gloves. The weight of the man suspended on the harness makes it come alive, thrumming like a super-sized guitar string and vibrating with his weight. And the sense of connection to the man in the harness is strong. We can't see him, of course, but we feel his mass, and there is a great physical release when he reaches the team at the top and scrambles away from the cliff edge. It isn't just that the tension leaves the rope entirely; along with it we lose our sense of connection to a living being. Within a minute or two, a new man will step into the harness unseen, and the rope will spring to life again.

A break is called, and we clamber back up the slope to sit together on the grass. Most of the men have already been retrieved from below, and there is a mound of lifeless birds piled up on the grass. Legs, feet, wings and long necks all jumble together into a shapeless mass of bedraggled feathers. The light is improving quickly, and another team of men take up station on the rope. Peering over the clifftop, I see Esbern walking up the sheer wall, one hand on the rope to steady himself while in the other he holds two large gannet chicks, one of which is mine...

Afterwards, I am unsettled, questioning whether I had been right to kill a gannet. I knew that the bird was doomed, and would have died by another hand within seconds if I had not used the knife. On one level, it seems a minor thing, but holding the warm, elegant creature in my hand had plunged me into a confrontation with hunting and death that was new and disconcerting.

Soon, in the creeping dawn, I see a straggle of figures making their way up to the clifftop from the track. Women are walking from the village, carrying flasks of tea and coffee, plastic beakers and dozens of warm pancakes wrapped in silver foil. The men revive again as the pancakes are unwrapped and there are jokes and chat and the smell of coffee in the morning air.

Word spreads that around 500 gannets have been killed, and that the next step is to wait for Jógvan Joensen to sail his boat *Hjalti* around the island to gather the carcases from below the cliffs. This involves a few men going back onto the ledge at Urðin, where some of the catch will be lowered to them by rope. These were the birds collected from the ledge known as Loftsrók, and they were tied together at the neck in bunches of five. Esbern and Jóhannus are among those who go down again, charged with hurling the carcases into the water.

I hear a mournful howl coming from the rocks below. Peering over the edge, I see a large rock a few hundred metres offshore, a skerry named Oysteinsfles, sheer-cut horizontally like a tree stump hewn with a chain-saw. The sound is being made by a bull seal, hauled out on the rocks. He wails like a lost spirit, the noise amplified into an echoing lament by the sea and the sheer cliff wall high above. The disembodied cry is somehow unearthly, and combined with the dawn atmosphere, makes me feel as if we are intruders into another, ancient time. All around the skerry and in the lee of Mykineshólmur as far out as I can see, the Atlantic is flat calm.

Soon, a little wooden boat putt-putts into view and stands off the cliff a little way. Then, grey missiles begin to hit the water. In death, the almost fledged gannets fly for the first and only time, cartwheeling through the morning air onto the hard flat sea with a resounding thwack. From where their now empty nests stand, a steady stream of adult birds cruise out above the water in their hundreds, circling and forming a gyre of white cruciform shapes made more brilliant by the rising sun.

Later that morning, everyone assembles back at the village jetty as the wooden fishing boat enters the narrow harbour and begins unloading the gannets. Esbern and some of the older men are in charge of counting and sorting the birds, which are grouped into separate piles for each of the eight separate landowners on Mykines. A further group is set aside for the boat's owner and then a larger communal pile for the men who had helped in the hunt. As part of the rope gang, I too will be given a share. A scientist from Faroes University is there too, and he selects several birds from the piles which he inspects for parasites and weighs – anything from three to four and a half kilograms. He explains to me that the gannet colony has been gradually increasing for a number of years, and the weight of the mature chicks seems to be holding steady. Birds are hefted in oily hands, bellies and breasts prodded and one by one they are passed between the men in charge who allocate them to one or other of the piles. The total catch is now known; 547 birds. That's been the steady average for the last few years. In the late 1930s, twice that number were taken, but some of the fowling spots used then are no longer accessible because of rock falls and gannets are not shot in winter as they once were.

In the full light of day, the birds cover the jetty and surroundings in a feathery carpet, errant wingtips sticking up into the air like tattered shark fins here and there. Soaked with seawater, the gannets are bedraggled, and each shows a gaping wound at the back of the skull where the spinal cord has been severed. They lie with their smooth graphite beaks tightly closed, their open eyes staring sightlessly at the metallic sky. But it is their feet, curling unnaturally at the end of their short sturdy legs, that strike me most. The webbing between their toes looks like withered autumn leaves. The skin is papery and lightly knobbled to the touch, reminding me of antique ladies' gloves made of pigskin, or perhaps something rarer, like the fine shagreen on the hilt of a Chinese sword that once belonged to my great-grandfather. As a boy, I had delighted in finding out that such leather was highly valued, as it allowed the holder to keep a tight grip even if the handle was covered in blood. The sword was part of a collection handed down to me from various members of the family; it included a 'Mau-Mau' spear from Kenya, my uncle's commando knife, a kukri from Borneo and several ceremonial regimental swords.

At last, Esbern gives the word and the men all rise, swarming over the rocks where the communal birds have been laid. They bend and squeeze the gannets' bellies, judging how fat they are, and thus how tasty. We are all entitled to two birds and I choose mine, following Jóhannus back up to the village where we have been invited to shelter in one of the small wooden houses until the ferry returns for the trip back to Vágar. We have a few hours yet to wait, and the Joensen brothers, Andor, Hilmar and Jesar, welcome us with tea, schnapps, cheese, chocolate, *skerpikjøt* and dried fish. I have never met any of them, but they accept me as if I am old friend. Andor's wife Bjørk is there too, along with their daughter Lóa, the only girl to go down the cliffs during the night. Just sixteen, I watched her send messages on her iPhone to friends back on the mainland, all the time wearing a hunting knife on a piece of string around her waist. Bjørk is welcoming and chatty, supplying me with constant tea while the others doze wherever they can find space in the small house, which is over a hundred years old. She is bright and cheerful, and one of those who got up in the small hours to make pancakes. Men drift in and out of her small kitchen, carving slivers of dried fermented mutton from the haunch on the table, or peeling a strip of dried fish from the pile on the breadboard. They all say they saw me on the cliffs, looking cold. Several people tell me I need to go and buy myself an *undirtroyggja*, the woollen undergarment which, combined with a Faroese sweater, is the best way to stay warm, whatever the weather. It is a lesson that has saved me much discomfort on excursions into the mountains since.

Bjørk is an artist, and she shows me photographs of her work, something she manages alongside her job as a hairdresser. Her paintings, created using her fingers rather than a brush, are on large canvases, many of them rich blue vistas inspired by the sea and the light around the islands. She also produces work based on the gannet colony on Mykines. Unsurprisingly, Faroese artists are frequently inspired by their wild and rugged natural environment. They accommodate an appreciation of the majesty and beauty of the animals and birds around them, with a belief that they are things which equally must be hunted, killed and eaten. Jesar, the youngest Joensen brother, reveals to me that his grandfather was a first cousin of the painter Sámal Joensen, the man who later took the name 'Mikines' as an artist.

On the ferry ride back to Vágar, the wind is stronger than it had been the day before and Tindhólmur looks forbidding as a light rain begins to fall. We all have our gannets in plastic bags on the deck at our feet. Once ashore, I give one of my birds to Jóhannus and the other to Benjámin, as thanks for lending me his hat.

The gannets are prized as an annual treat in Faroes now, and the following day, Jóhannus invites me to his parents' house to learn how to prepare the birds for cooking. The gannets are hanging outside when I arrive, impaled on hooks inserted in the backs of their skulls. We pluck the birds, clearing the chests and bellies of their newly sprouted feathers and leaving a covering of fine fluffy white down. After gutting them and removing the outer half of their wings (which have almost no meat upon them), Jóhannus shows me how to singe the remaining down from the bodies with a gas-powered blow-torch, after which we have to rub them over with a kitchen scourer to remove the follicles. Then it is time for another go on the blow-torch, and more scouring, with the whole process repeated three or four times. I remember seeing film of the Hebridean guga hunters singeing off the feathers over an open fire. The plucked, headless and limbless carcases now look just like any fowl ready for the oven. There is no vestige of the elegant seabirds that clustered on the cliffs of Mykines. They will be roasted over many hours in a dish lined with a deep bed of salt to absorb the fat that oozes from the carcase. They will taste sweet, a little like duck cooked well, but with none of its dryness.

Ravens IX

Mid June

There is a lamb entangled in the sheep fence on the farm track. Somehow it has weaved one back leg through not one, but three of the square wire openings. It's lying in a deep puddle with its legs splayed, and panting with rapid shallow gasps. There's no way of knowing how long it's been lying there – perhaps all night. It has just enough strength to buck and struggle weakly as I grab it and manoeuvre the leg out of the wire, getting comprehensively sprayed with mud. It takes a few minutes to disentangle, and when it finally hobbles off, one leg drags limply behind. It bleats furiously, but there is no answering call from its mother. After a few minutes, the lamb gingerly puts it foot to the ground. At first it walks with a pronounced limp, and I wonder if I should call the shepherd, but soon enough it bounds up the mountainside seemingly none the worse for wear.

No raven flies above the fjord this morning, a warm clear day with a light breeze. The sun polishes the sea, and the land is rich in green and gold like a silk carpet. It is low tide and the eiders are congregating at the mouth of the gorge. I watch them for half an hour before ascending the slope to check on the nest. One of the chicks is gone. I feel panicked.

I quickly crawl to the ravine edge and peer down as best I can towards the water, imagining it might have fallen on one of its pecking expeditions around the niche. It seems entirely possible that it could have slipped off the rockface, or even tried to fly for the first time and crashed into the sea. I climb higher, to the upper slope, and scan the water with my binoculars, and then walk back down to sea level. The water is flat calm and there is no sign of a dead bird. With the binoculars, I eventually spot a raven strutting about on the southern point at the other side of the chasm. It's too far to tell if it's a chick or not, so I begin walking in the same direction, skirting the hazardously steep landward end of the gorge and negotiating the sheep-rutted slopes along the cliff. These tiny hoofmarks ripple and rib the land.

There is no man-made path here, just occasional furrows where the grass is worn down and the earth ridged in a narrow track where the sheep have taken the easiest route around a dip in the land, or down the sides of a gully. My booted foot is wide, and clumsy, and I need to concentrate, aware that haste could be disastrous. A deeper ravine cuts through the outfield and drops vertiginously towards the sea a few hundred metres from where the ravens nest. It has a river within it, with pools just big enough to bathe in, and steep sides where loose rocks and red earth slip and slide underfoot. I am breathless as I scramble down to the river bed, through the shallow water and back up on the other side to regain the sheep track in the outfield. Off to my right hand side, the high mountain ridge makes a barrier for me, or any novice raven chick not yet able to fly properly. Across the water, the rump of Koltur is now clearly visible to the south, but, after an hour of scanning the land and sea, I find no ravens.

I turn inland to retrace my steps, crossing an open amphitheatre below the looming ridge that blocks the way to the west of the island. Two birds are locked in a wheeling aerial chase in the far distance. They soar and plummet in a tight dance, so close they could be tethered together by a piece of string. With binoculars, I can see that it's an Arctic skua harassing an Arctic tern. Unlike great skuas, the Arctic variety doesn't kill the smaller bird, but chases it until it lets go of whatever fish it has caught. The skua is twice its size, but the tern drops and banks in tight circles. Its long arching wings seem to allow it to stall mid-air, and then swerve past the bigger bird. After a furious minute of this frenetic ballet, the tern swoops very low, skimming the ground as it passes me, breaking for the open fjord. The skua gives chase half-heartedly, before opening its wings to land heavily on the grass, beak agape.

I climb towards the sun and a waterfall. I am half a kilometre inland now, and high above the sea. There is a stream ahead and beyond it the ground is uneven, and a low stony ridge blocks my view to the mountain behind. As I clamber across the loose bed of the stream, I need to use my hands to scramble up the far bank. Like a soldier emerging from the trenches, I'm just about to haul myself over the top, when I spy movement in the grass just a few metres away. A raven.

Somehow I know it must be the chick and my heart leaps. I rest below the lip of the gully, poking my head up cautiously to watch the bird hopping through the summer grass. There is a pure energy in the way it bounces along, investigating the ground with its beak, clearly looking for food.

With binoculars, I can tell that it has a ring on its leg, and I can make out the number 092, confirming it's one of my chicks and must have left the nest this morning. I am ecstatic. I emerge from the ravine on all fours, and then stoop to walk obliquely in the same direction as the raven. It has seen me, but it doesn't noticeably alter its pace or behaviour. Up ahead, a snipe takes flight with a warm thrumming of tail feathers and fast beating wings silhouetted against blue sky. I wonder if 092 will find its nest, perhaps with an egg inside it.

Slowly, cautiously, and with my head down, avoiding eye contact, I get within five metres of the raven. Then, invading its space, I cross an invisible barrier, and it opens its wings in all their glossy brilliance. Still, the bird does not fly, but manages a hop, skip and jump away from me. I move towards it once more, taking my time, and it retreats again, now jumping into the air and making a short glide of no more than two or three metres down the sloping ground. I don't want to frighten it any more, and I back off, lying down on the grass to watch as it continues its quick bouncing progress towards the narrow ridge ahead. The basalt is like a rampart, a fitting refuge for this handsome black knight.

10

The Gathering

The new sheepdog is missing. His name is Cap and he's only been on the island three weeks, a recent very valuable purchase brought over from Holland by one of the landowners. Tórbjørn Poulsen made the long car and sea journey via Denmark to buy him for another farmer, and he was expensive because he's a fully trained four-year-old. The trouble is, he's not used to an island like Mykines, and its steep cliffs and roaring winds. No one saw the fall, but Esbern thinks Cap went over the edge near the ramshackle storehouses on the promontory above the jetty. In the old days, it was the place where they tipped rubbish into the sea thirty metres below. It's mid-October and a near-gale is blowing from the south-west with surf four or five metres high smashing into rocks that are as unforgiving as the wind. Looking down into the fast churning water makes me dizzy as it swirls and rolls, the incoming waves glistening brightly as they arch against the light.

From the clifftop, Esbern and I scan the water repeatedly with our binoculars. We both spot it at the same time: something rolling in the surf, black, shapeless and distinctly out of place in the water. It ducks swiftly beneath the frothing surface and then a minute later it reappears, a crumpled matted thing. But it's just a fleece from one of the slaughtered sheep. 'No dog,' says Esbern quietly. 'I think he's gone.'

The whole western end of Mykines is being scoured, with men on quad-bikes racing to the high ground and even climbing down steep sheep tracks on the northern edge of the island to check the dog could not have fallen somehow onto a ledge and been unable to climb back up. Tórbjørn is one of those out with a rope, and I can hear him whistling and calling somewhere far below, out of sight on one of the thin paths carved by the sheep. He tells me to stay with Esbern as he doesn't want me slipping and following the dog into the sea.

Esbern says he too has lost a dog here, and in the coming days other shepherds tell me they have seen experienced animals go over the edge when chasing tough Faroese sheep, which defy gravity and that almost constant wind as they cling to the seaward edges of these islands. A friend on another island tells me he once had a dog that had been trained to grab sheep by the fleece to turn them. One day, his dog seized a large ram close to the cliff edge and the ram spun around quickly, shaking the dog off and sending it over the edge into the sea twenty metres below. Miraculously, it survived the fall and began swimming along the coast, looking for landfall. The sea wasn't rough, but there was nowhere accessible to get ashore and the man had no rope with which he could climb down. He followed the dog as it swam along the coast for more than an hour, watching helplessly and hoping it might find some foothold, but it eventually tired and drowned. On Mykines, the search goes on: we look in the basements of empty houses, in the sheep pens and the stone shelters on the moor, out on the *hólm* and in the ravines and gullies all around the nearby stretches of coast. There is no sign of Cap, and after more than a day of searching, everyone agrees that he's become a casualty of the cliffs.

I am staying with Tórbjørn in his wooden house at the edge of the village. Tummas Henriksen, who runs the ferry to Mykines, and his wife Maja are there too. Maja's cousin Jákup Heri (who happens to be Tórbjørn's brother-in-law) has also come to help with the round-up. I'm the outsider, but more men will come over on the helicopter over the next few days, weather permitting. Tórbjørn says around eight people are needed to catch the sheep. There are just over 1000 ewes on Mykines altogether, and around a quarter of them live in Borgardalur, the vast valley on the eastern edge of the island, cut off from the village by the high ridge at Knúkur.

Tórbjørn knows every ripple in the land on Mykines. In herding season, he stays in the family log cabin built by his father-in-law forty years ago at the edge of the village. Out on the cliffs, he is usually accompanied only by his Border collies, Kelly and Daisy. Today he is heading for the southern edge of the island, to a rocky spur named Innaranes below the high cliffs that drop down from the wide-open heights of Líðarhagi. On its short journey from Vágar, the helicopter often flies along this coastline, giving spectacular views of the rumpled folding land. I have stared at it from the air, and been told that men herd sheep here, but always find it impossible to see where anyone could walk safely on the slopes. They seem utterly sheer, barely fit for sheep but surely impassable on two legs. As we climb the rise to the east of the village, Tórbjørn asks me how I feel about heights. 'You can wait at the top,' he says. 'But I'll be gone a few hours and you may get cold.'

He walks quickly and carries nothing except for a pair of binoculars and a traditional Faroese wooden crook with a decoratively carved tip, like some mythical staff. Tórbjørn is slim and pale with hair the colour of a silver harvest moon, and narrow metal-framed glasses. He seems ageless, with unblemished skin and boyish energy, though I know he has grown-up children. In the early evening, he eats a hearty cooked dinner, but often goes out onto the hills without any breakfast.

There's no actual path where we are heading, just the spongy ground that skirts a series of indentations in the side of the island where the ground falls progressively more steeply into the sea. The sheep's hooves have done their customary work of marking their own tracks along the way, but the ground is so acutely angled that one misplaced step and I would slide over the edge into the watery abyss. I long ago gave up wearing modern water-proof fabrics, having been warned by Faroese friends that they would make me slide faster down the grassy inclines if I fell. Waxed cotton is safer, and I have a walking pole that I can plant firmly into the ground. I lean inwards as we pick our way along the coast, and Tórbjørn slows his pace to accommodate me and checks regularly that I am OK. In general, I've learned that he's not prone to idle chit-chat. But as we pause to let me catch my breath, he makes a rare unprompted statement. 'This is the best time in the world. Being alone with my dogs and looking for the sheep. I feel like I could stay out here for ever.' He says it unselfconsciously and doesn't expect me to respond. And then he's off again, with Daisy and Kelly running just ahead, ears up and on the alert for sheep.

After a kilometre or so, the grass gives way to a band of rich red scree littered with boulders. I am forced to crouch low and use my stick, making a conscious effort to move only one leg at a time, having the other and the stick firmly planted before taking the next step. Small stones dislodged by my boots skitter downwards, gathering speed and bouncing in increasingly high arcs as they hurtle towards edge and then make their final arching fall into the water 200 metres below. 'Do you want to go further?' Tórbjørn asks. As long as I don't focus on the drop into the sea I am OK, and I decide to continue. 'There's a place ahead that's flatter where you can wait,' he says. 'It'll get harder after that.'

The flat spot is called Heimaranes, a thick green buttress overlooking a bay marked on the map as Smørbúshellisgjógv The ground evens out for a way and is strewn with boulders that have come down from the escarpment above. We are only about a hundred metres above the sea here, but the cliffs behind climb a further three hundred to the great plateau above, the place where the Icelandair plane crashed fifty years ago. Tórbjørn heads off with the dogs and disappears around the next headland. For a time I can hear him calling to the dogs, and then there is nothing but the sound of the surf hitting the rocky foreshore below. I feel sure it's right that I stay where I'm not an extra burden for him on the steepest part of the coast.

Alone on the cliffs, I can just make out the dim smudgy outline of Suðuroy, two hours south from Tórshavn by ferry. A great skua passes overhead and swings down to inspect me, but otherwise this is an isolated place. The wind is from the east and it's bitterly cold, forcing me into the lee of some boulders, but even lying flat on the ground behind the rocks it's impossible to find shelter. I bury my hands in my coat pockets and pull my woollen hat down low. Eventually, more than two hours after Tórbjørn set off, I see movement on the path to the east. He is driving about a dozen rams towards me, with Daisy and Kelly flanking them, one dog high and the other lower on the steep ground to stop them breaking away. I scamper ahead, as fast as I can, anxious not to scare the animals back the way they have come, making it up to the plateau a few minutes ahead of the herd. Tórbjørn pauses with them at the fence that keeps the rams separated from the ewes on the plateau. It's the only barrier before we head down towards the village. 'Did you find them all?' I ask. 'No, there were a couple of rams that went out on a ledge and it was too dangerous to catch them,' he replies. 'But I will get them next time.'

As we cut down the steep southern edge of the island towards Mykines, Tórbjørn constantly gives commands to the dogs, especially five-year-old Kelly, who seems to be his favourite. 'She is clever,' he says. 'She knows where we are going now.' The sheep are calm and move steadily downhill, the colours of their wool lit by the sinking sun. None of the rams have pure-white fleeces, although it's common enough to see a sheep which is pure black all over. They can range from steely grey to warm russet, some with a necklace of one colour and a head and body of another. Some have white faces with black patches and some have a front half entirely black and a rear half entirely white, as if they have been dipped head first into a vat of ink. There are sheep with red socks and white socks, black socks and those with single or double socks of different colours. More than 300 different fleece patterns are recognised in Faroes, and no matter the colour combination of the parents, no one can predict how the lambs will look.

Come late October there will be *seyðasýning*, regional shows, for rams from all over the islands, where they will be judged for size and colour, horn shape, wool quality and comportment. Straight legs are especially valued, but Tórbjørn tells me ruefully that Mykines rams never do well in the national competition because their legs are rarely good enough. The animals which do best will go forward to the national competition, the *Landsseyðasýning* which is more about honour than any cash prize for the farmers.

Back on Mykines, Tórbjørn herds the sheep into a pen outside the village, and several of the older men amble across the fields to see the rams he has brought in. There is Eddie Lauritsen, Jákup í Løðu and Reðin Leonson, all year-round residents of the island. They have woollen hats and well-worn Faroese sweaters, and as they lean against the sheep pen fence, they chat about the animals. It's decided they will return in the morning to weigh and inspect them. For now the sheep will go into pens inside the barn and huddle together for the night. As we close the door and walk the short distance across the field to the village, I realise it's past six and Tórbjørn hasn't eaten since breakfast even though he's walked fifteen kilometres or more to gather the sheep. Reðin announces he has some *ræst kjøt* and potatoes for our dinner boiling now in his bright-yellow painted house near to Tórbjørn's cabin. 'Come!' Tórbjørn says, breaking into a trot. 'Let's get changed and go!'

* * *

Today is the day on Mykines when most of the sheep in Borgardalur must be herded back to the village for the autumn sorting and slaughter. Extra men and dogs flew in with the helicopter yesterday to help and we all set out after breakfast for the high pass. From the ridgeline above the plain I can see no sheep on the sweeping open ground below me, and Tórbjørn says the men will have to fan out and drop down over the edge of the plain to the cliffs and shelving pasture at the margins of the island to find them. Tummas and his wife Maja are heading to the northern side while Tórbjørn is going for the far southern edge of Borgardalur. Tórhallur and Eddie go straight ahead through the valley to the narrow tip of the island. Everyone will meet back in the middle and try to drive whatever sheep they can gather in a herd towards the high ground. Guarding the top of the pass is Jákup Heri, who has driven one of the ATVs to the lip of the ridge and will wait for the group to return. In the valley there will be five dogs altogether, including Kelly and Daisy. I follow Eddie down the scree track through the pass and along a rough stony path which peters out at the edge of a knee-jarring descent across the sheep ruts all the way down to the valley floor. I veer off northwards as Eddie presses on with his dogs, Rose, Glen and Flora.

I revel in the empty space. There is no clamour of seabirds here, but every few hundred metres I put up a snipe which disturbs the stillness of the valley. A few giant boulders sit in water-filled depressions in the mossy sward, miniature castle keeps with their own tiny moat. On their southern faces there is lichen flaking like drying scabs and I climb onto one as big as a double bed to get a longer view. A toothy rim of strange jagged outcrops decorates the southern edge of the valley walls; they are gnarled sculptural shapes, and they remind me of grotesque Punch and Judy puppets with jutting chins and noses covered in warts. There is a sense of pure open space. It's cold as usual, but the light is strong.

The ewes roam in loose groups, an ebb and flow of movement, making patterns indistinct and abstract along the valley floor. Every now and then, they clump together like iron filings drawn by a magnet, then scatter again. As they approach the thin scree slope leading up to Knúkur from the valley, I can pick out individuals; browns and greys, whites and blacks, speckled and piebald, each one an unrepeatable patchwork of colours. The shepherds stay back, thirty metres or more from the rear of the herd, each man a point on an arc that tightens as they approach the pass. Everyone except Tórbjørn is on the valley floor; he has climbed high up the northern rim to cut off any sheep which might try to climb the escarpment wall into neighbouring Kálvadalur. I can see him squatting on his haunches up there with Kelly beside him, both of them watching the action below.

There is a gentle and constant chorus of noise as the herd approaches. Ewes give out a short sharp call, and the lambs bleat back. I am crouched behind boulders right at the pass neck, staying still and low so as not to spook any sheep back down the slope. Some walk by without noticing me, while others stop and stare at me for a moment, especially the lambs, but after a second or two they carry on, following their leaders up and on to the high ground. Once up there, with the shepherds and dogs behind them, they can only go straight ahead. The challenge is keeping them from spreading out across the whole width of the plateau. Tórbjørn explains that we will drive them past Knúkur and then once down on the plain, veer north a little way to Heimangjógv, to avoid the steep descent we made with the rams. Then we will follow the river course down to the entrance to the village where there is a large field in which they can be penned.

It's almost six and we have been out since ten this morning. The animals move steadily along, and on this final downward slope we must trot to keep up with them. As we approach the valley floor and hit the track beside the river, we are heading directly into the setting sun. We are still under a cornflower sky but out at sea there is a squall coming, a dark curtain suspended over the tip of Mykineshólmur and the nearby stacks where the gannets nest. I watch the rain fall in the west as a flaming shower of light joining the dark cloud to the sea.

*   *   *

It is the time of slaughter. The sheep are brought from the field in batches to the pens at the north end of the village. On this grisly morning, they skitter and slip over the wet rocky ground in the holding area before being separated into batches; rams, ewes and lambs. The farmers handle them confidently but gently, pulling down their bottom lip to check their front teeth – a good way of aging a sheep, as they produce adult incisors in pairs with each successive year. Just like us, the growing sheep replace their milk teeth; at one year they have a single pair of permanent incisors and at two, two pairs. At four they have the total complement of four pairs. The upper jaw has no teeth at the front, just a hard ridged palate against which the grass torn off by the incisors is crushed. It's then ground down by the twenty-four molars well back in the jaw. The sheep have strong little tongues which feel rubbery to the touch. Male lambs are examined with a hand between the back legs to check the testicles are present, while ewes have their udders squeezed to see if they are bearing milk.

All of the sheep are weighed, on a primitive contraption consisting of a metal cradle balanced on a wooden pole. The sheep is lifted onto the cradle and a man grasps the pole to bear the weight as it is raised a few inches off the ground. There is much talk of fleece and horns, of weight and age. A good ram will be anything from forty to sixty kilograms live-weight, and a ewe barely half that. The meat from the carcases will be slightly less than half the live-weight. Sheep here are not aged in years, but in winters. Older ewes are examined to see if they have reached the end of their useful breeding age, usually around five or six winters, occasionally a little more. I learn to spot the great-great-great-grandmother ewes, with their scraggy wool, thin cheeks and broken mouths, and generally less muscular bodies.

The slaughter time is in some ways the end of the farming year, and in other ways a beginning. The peak time for gathering the sheep and slaughtering is throughout October, depending on weather and the availability of the men. On Stóra Dímun, they get a head start on the other islands by slaughtering in September, partly because until recently it was thought wise to have your meat ready for sale before the bad weather set in, so that the carcases and wool could still be safely taken off the island by boat. The lambs there are also born a little earlier too, because they let their rams run free with the ewes after the autumn round-up, instead of keeping them indoors until December. Ewes in a flock come into heat at roughly the same time – a process triggered in Faroes by the shortening daylight hours in October. In many areas it has become common for breeding rams to be kept indoors in the autumn and only put out with the ewes in December so that lambs will be born at the end of April or early May, when the weather may be kinder. If the rams are let loose, they will use precious energy asserting dominance and be in poor strength for a harsh winter. On Dímun, there is significantly less snow than on most of the other islands and Janus úr Dímun tells me that his rams seem to survive the winter well enough. His youngest ewes – the *gimburlombini*, which may be too small and too young to breed in their first spring, are protected by a traditional contraceptive device which is attached to their hind quarters when they are brought in at the round-up. Janus patiently taught me how to do it. Holding the ewe in a headstall, I straddle her back, facing her tail. With a needle and thread I sew a patch – called a *bót* – into the thick wool on her rump, using a simple cross stitch so that it hangs down over her anus and vulva, in such a way that it doesn't impede bodily functions but prevents penetration by the rams. Now, a rectangle of thick plastic is used for the *bót* but in the old days it would have been a piece of sacking or just a rag.

On Mykines, Tórbjørn is slaughtering some rams tonight for Jákup. Half a dozen have been moved into a small raised pen in a farm building in the middle of the village. The wooden interior is musty with animal smells and every surface is crammed with tools, waterproofs and overalls. There are oil cans and balls of twine, pliers and cable-ties, coffee mugs and an old kettle sitting beside a sink. There is a tap on the wall with a hosepipe attached and the floor is roughly cast concrete. The space – about eight metres long – is lit by fluorescent tubes shaded with square plastic panels that diffuse the light. In the centre of the hut stand two wooden trestles. Sturdily made of wood, they resemble something you might find in an hotel bedroom to rest your suitcase on, except the slatted top surface is at waist height and is scalloped to accommodate not luggage, but a sheep's carcase. Known as *flettingarborð*, they are where the sheep are spreadeagled for butchering.

Tórbjørn asks me to fetch the first ram so I climb up into the gloomy pen at one end of the room where they are all huddled together in the corner. They are all going to be slaughtered tonight, so there is no merit in choosing one animal over another. I grasp a grey-fleeced animal and manoeuvre it towards the door, where I hold it firmly between my knees with one horn in each hand. Tórbjørn has the killing tool, a solidly machined cylinder of steel about the size of a kitchen hand blender primed with an explosive cartridge. He places the base of the tool carefully in the centre of the animal's skull and presses the side-mounted trigger. To kill a ram the bolt gun must be placed behind the thick bony ridge just above the horns, while with ewes you aim at an area slightly more forward on the skull. The sound is not the explosive bang of a gun, more like that of a heavy paperback book being slapped down on a hard surface. The cartridge causes a captive bolt about four centimetres long to shoot from the cylinder, piercing the skull and penetrating the brain. Between my knees, the sheep's legs buckle and it drops instantly. Tórbjørn seizes it and manhandles it straight onto the *flettingarborð*. There is no gaping wound – the hole in its skull obscured by the thick wool – and no blood. The ram's head hangs down over the edge of the trestle, eyes open and pupils fixed wide. The iris is the colour of golden agate.

Tórbjørn has a knife with a six-inch blade. He pushes it into the ram's throat, behind the windpipe, and flexes it a little from side to side to cut the main blood vessels, then forces it all the way through the skin on the neck on the other side. A stream of blood gushes onto the floor, splattering our boots and the shins of our oilskins. It is the deepest purest shade of summer-poppy red. The ram's legs twitch and make violent galloping movements in the air as the warm blood leaves the muscles. In less than half a minute, the twitching stops and the blood flow ceases. He tilts its chin back and saws through the space between the skull and the top vertebra. The wool gives way to the sharp knife with a soft tearing noise, and he passes me the head to place on a stepladder leaning against the wall.

By the end of the night there will be two rams' heads on each rung. The mouths hang loose, the tongues protrude a little and the open eyes stare sightlessly ahead. The horns will be sawn off and when the time is right the heads will be scorched to remove the fleece and boiled for a few hours with potatoes. They are eaten as a treat. I find them very strong in flavour, and there is always a lump of fatty gristle at the back of the skull that is unpalatable. The cheeks and the tongue are the most edible parts, but a grown man needs at least two heads to make a decent meal.

With the head removed, Tórbjørn makes a shallow incision in the ram's skin down the centre line of the throat, then in a Y shape down one foreleg and finally back across the chest and down the other foreleg. He swiftly breaks the leg joints and cuts off the front feet. He passes them to me to put in a bucket under the sink. He flips the carcase over and inserts his fingers under the skin at the open neck. This is the process they call *tumma* – the gradual loosening of the fleece from the underlying tissue. It is crucial to producing a smooth unblemished carcase which can hang in the *hjallur* for the drying and fermentation process. I watch as he inserts his fists under the skin, kneading with his knuckles and loosening the outer skin from the fine thin layer of tissue that covers the muscle underneath. He moves his balled fists down the torso, now and then pausing to rinse his hands under a running tap to make them slide more easily under the fleece. Tórbjørn is flushed with the effort, pink in the face. I watch his fingers under the wool and flinch as I see his hand, like a subcutaneous worm, reach around the testicles and rip the testes from inside their furry pouch, leaving it saggy and empty. Only when the fleece has been loosened all the way to the rump does he take the knife and split the skin down the mid-line of the chest. He peels it back like an open cardigan and the pink naked carcase sits exposed. Under the tube lights steam rises from the still-warm belly. Then, Tórbjørn takes his knife and cuts the skin around the ankles of the rear legs and removes the feet. The bones crack like kindling. To free the skin and wool from the underlying tissue, he cuts around the penis and then amputates the fatty skin around the tail. Then the body is pulled free of the fleece, leaving only the rear legs still attached. The exposed tail bone is thin and meagre, unappealing and rat-like. The next stage is to slice down the neck vertically, a shallow meticulous cut to expose the oesophagus and trachea. A final short stabbing motion to one side of the trachea penetrates the sac around the heart and releases a short spurt of blackening blood. The breathing tube shines white and gristly, while the food tube is a slimy dirty brown colour. He pulls them through the open cut in the throat and ties them in a knot to prevent undigested food from leaking out and contaminating the meat.

Jákup enters the hut and exchanges a few words with Tórbjørn. He will disembowel and gut the sheep while Tórbjørn slaughters and skins the next. Over the coming days, I get familiar with the internal parts of the sheep. The caul fat, elastic as an old string shopping bag, will be stretched around a mound of colon fat and left to solidify so that it can be shaved into slices and melted down later in the winter as *garnatálg*. The stomach muscles will be used for making rolled meat – *rullupylsa*, and the thin slimy rectum used to make *sperðil* sausage. The lungs, heart and liver, collectively known as the *mørur*, are left joined to one another and hang, still attached to their tracheas from convenient nails on the barn walls. My hands and boots and trousers are covered with fat and blood. I watch the fresh red streams gather and congeal, at first into shining red gobbets, gooey and viscous between my fingers. But then within minutes they magically separate into fine strands like piles of crocheted yarn, a tangle of wormlike structures which solidify and dry, grainy and soft to the touch.

As the days go by, we gradually add to the lines of cleaned carcasses that hang from hooks in the ceiling at the other end of the slaughterhouse. The rams yet to be slaughtered are at one end of the room, impassive and uncomprehending, so far as I can tell, in their gloomy stall, waiting their turn.

Ravens X

Late June

On the grass near my hiding place, there is a raven's feather. The short stubby quill is transparent, but where it narrows and curves elegantly away into the shaft it darkens, merging and matching the barbs. Up close, this tight weft shows a swathe of iridescence, a shimmering shadow within the feather that has the colour and lustre of a ripe purple grape. The chicks are already gone and the nest is a crumbling tower. The gorge belongs to the fulmars now. I return whenever I can, in the hope of finding any of the three young ravens in the outfield, but they seem to have moved on. There is no sign of the adult pair on the headland today, though they are probably still feeding the chicks and teaching them how to forage. The land looks empty, but there are oystercatchers and whimbrels aplenty snuggled in the grass, still guarding chicks. This is the time for fungi too, and 'witch's cap' toadstools have sprung up near to the steep ravine where the river has slowed to half its normal width. They are deep oxblood red, visceral and clammy, viscous and sticky topped.

Heading for the high ground, I explore the basalt ridge where I last saw the fledged chick. In the stream bed, small darting birds sound the alarm as I scramble across. They are wheatears, small as robins, with a quick bouncing low-level flight. They are birds to make you smile, somehow hopeful and cheerful in their wave-like progress above the grass. Like the gannets, these little birds will retreat to Africa for the northern winter.

Today is one of those late-June days when I have no desire to be anywhere further south. No tropical beach or equatorial mountain ridge could shine more brightly than this northern island. It is close to high summer, and the fjord is a glistening ribbon of royal-blue silk framed by the smooth haunches of Vágar and Streymoy. I choose a spot on the high ground, where I can hear the soft fizz of the waterfall hitting the surface of the sound. The fine spray is backlit by the morning sun and made into a gleaming diamond-bright spout.

Something is moving in the channel. First, it's just a rippling outline, and then a smooth pale shape emerges at the surface, and I recognise the head of a seal. It flips onto its back, flipper hands bony and awkward, clasping a fish in its claws. The seal's bullet head is large, certainly a male judging by the elongated jaw. His nose is long and strong, so pugnaciously dog-like it reminds me of an English bull terrier. He takes his time, manipulating the fish on his chest and leaning forward to pluck at the flesh, tearing it off in long strips with his teeth. Nearby, a black guillemot floats by, unconcerned. Occasionally the seal sinks below the water, rinsing the fish mess from his body, before resurfacing to resume his meal. The fish is large and red-scaled, and it takes the seal more than five minutes to consume it. He dives again, and I think he has gone. Then, there is the tell-tale ripple, and I catch sight of a submarine ghost heading back to the mouth of the gorge. The glistening head appears, thick strong whiskers clearly visible at the snout as he stands vertically in the water, turning on the spot to look all around him. Then, he swims towards the waterfall and positions himself directly under the spout. For some time, he lies on his back again, letting the fresh water bounce off his torso. He rolls and ducks, slowly, gracefully, returning to let the stream play on his head as if he were under a bathroom shower. After a few minutes, he rolls sideways and streaks away towards the deeper water, torpedoing just below the surface of the fjord so that I can see his bow-wave heading into mid-channel. I watch until he is lost in other gentle offshore shadows.

Further along the coast I see movement. A black bird hugs the shoreline, deep full-chested wingbeats marking a steady rhythm. I know it must be a raven, long before it is close enough to be sure. Just a short distance from the ravine, it breaks inland and flies right across my line of sight. It's carrying something in its half-open beak. They say here that only ravens can find the *sigursteinur* – a magical amulet that makes the wearer invincible. A closer view reveals that all this bird has is a large white egg, stolen, I suspect, from a gull. The raven flies inland, keeping low and skimming the hummocked ground towards the basalt ridge, where I hope at least one of my adolescent chicks will share the egg's light golden heart.

11

Blue Hares

Today is the first day of hare-hunting season, and as we set off on foot from the hamlet of Bøur at first light, the water in Sørvágsfjørður glows like mackerel skin. Jóhannus scrambles over a waist-high dry-stone wall beside the road and sets off on a steep track leading up the mountainside. I follow, not quite so nimbly. We both have rucksacks with food and extra clothing and he has a 12-gauge shotgun across his shoulders. Parts of the island have snow on the high ground now, a fine sprinkling that makes the smooth humped hills resemble gigantic choux pastries dusted with icing sugar. As we climb higher I can see house lights twinkling in Sørvágur in the distance. Beyond, to the east, I can just make out the glint of Faroes' largest lake, Sørvágsvatn, the stretch of freshwater close to the airport that plunges over the cliffs into the sea in a tremendous cataract. With the summer birds long gone, the silence of the mountains is almost a solid physical presence. The November land is quiet, sinking into a regenerative slumber after the high activity of summer and the autumn herding of the sheep.

Silhouetted against the sky almost 400 metres above

the village, other men gather, waiting for us to catch up. They are all part of the syndicate that shares shooting rights here, on the mountain heights called Tormanshagi. Tórbjørn the shepherd is there, and he and Jóhannus reel off the introductions: Tórhallur, Zacharis, Brandur, Ove, Helgi and Jón. Everyone wears a high-vis vest and bright orange hat for safety. In total, there will be eight guns, and I am here on condition I stay close behind Jóhannus and keep up with the group as they string out in a line abreast, each man about a hundred metres away from his neighbour.

The men are looking for *Lepus timidus*, otherwise known as mountain or blue hares, a species common across the northern hemisphere as far south as Italy and as far east as Japan. A trio of hares was imported from the Telemark region of Norway in 1855, and several more were brought in over the next few years. The idea was to bring another food resource to Faroes, and now they inhabit fifteen of the eighteen islands. They have adapted well to the high ground here, and have no natural predators. They are a sub-species now; it was noticed quite soon after they came to Faroes that they no longer grew pure-white winter coats, as they did in Norway, perhaps because the maritime climate here means that snow is less reliable, and the animals are better camouflaged against the rocky slopes by turning from their summer brown to silvery-blue in winter.

Tormanshagi is rugged land. And the climb upwards is relentless until we reach a sweeping escarpment overlooking a small heart-shaped lake. The winter sun gives it the dull shine of antique pewter. Jón asks if the climb is hard work. 'A bit,' I pant, as we pause for a rest. 'Don't worry, it's hard for us Faroese too,' he smiles. He is tall and handsome with neatly trimmed blond stubble, and a gentle manner.

This area is just one of more than 450 outfields in Faroes, and these high empty fells of Vágar are one of the best places to find hares. The ground is stony and nothing grows more than a few inches high. A steely wind whips in from the west, and I pull up my collar, glad for once that I have gloves in my pocket. It's around five degrees but the wind makes it feel much colder. Below the high ridge the grass on the hillsides and in the valleys is a mixture of green and gold, the mellow glow of autumn gradually taking over from the lush shoots of summer. We walk across a tongue of exposed scree below the 600-metre peak of Snældansfjall. A light rain begins to fall. Jón is off to our left higher up the mountainside, and Tórhallur to the right. The ground up here is ribbed with exposed rock and strewn with boulders. It seems a barren place, and it's hard to imagine anything choosing to live up here.

When the first shot rings out, it splits the air like a bull-whip. A sharp reverberation rattles off the hard rocks. Two more in quick succession: *crack! crack!* The sound comes from my left and Jóhannus quickens his pace, loping across the boulder field as sure-footedly as one of his sheep, his gun slung low and gripped with both hands, barrel pointing downwards. His head remains steady and his back straight as he runs, and he brings the shotgun up in a quick fluid movement without pause. There is the rich *thwop* of the 12-gauge as he fires. I see a hare racing straight towards us across the crumbling scree, and as it breaks to his left, Jóhannus spins on his heels with the gun still pressed to his cheek. *Thwop*. And again. *Thwop*. The animal cartwheels full circle, once, twice before it hits the ground. He is on it in seconds, grabbing it by the hind legs and jogging back to where I stand. 'Here,' he says, passing me the animal before jogging away again. 'We must keep up with the line!' Then I see that the first of his three shots was also successful and he shouts for me to pick up the other carcase as I pass. I have two animals now to carry, and I can examine them up close for the first time. Their feet and soft underbellies are cotton-wool white, like their tails, but the fur on the rest of the small warm bodies is wolf grey, as delicately shaded as a brooding rain cloud. The eyes are large and dark – decidedly not amber – and there are other differences with the brown hares I know from England. There, I have seen them in the spring lying doggo in the grass when they have leverets to protect, one hare immobile while its mate takes off across the fields, distracting any nearby predators. My dog Dipper can catch most things, but he never gets near a running hare. These Faroese hares have rounder, less bony, much more bunny-rabbit-shaped faces than *Lepus europaeus*. But, like the hares I have seen crouched still and low in the grass at home, their ears are tipped with a fine line of black hair all around the delicately curved rim. The ears are much less elongated in relation to the skull, which is itself shorter from brow to snout. The pelt blends perfectly with the rocky ground and even the bright white tails merge with the patches of pale lichen on the boulders.

The line of men moves steadily across the bare flat land, and comes to a halt at Gapið, a ridge 500 metres above a steep drop off from where I can now see the Atlantic dead ahead. The men are gathered in a group and there is talk about which direction they will take next. Jóhannus says I must be sure to keep up with the line on the steep ground to avoid spoiling anyone's shot. Jón confesses he fired three or four times but only got one hare. The group know each other well, and they follow a pattern worked out over the years to maximise the way they cover the shooting range. We are to head for Snældansgil, a ravine cutting east from the mountain behind us, and then towards a spot they call Túgvan. A couple of the men will go ahead and then circle, driving any hares from the north back towards the line. Helgi reminds everyone to be doubly sure that their line of sight is clear before they shoot.

After giving the advance party a few minutes to get into position, it is time to move again. The ground drops away steeply, and we scramble downwards more than a hundred metres. I watch my footing, fearful of twisting an ankle and embarrassing myself. There is the regular *crack-crack* of the shotguns as we go. The hares run towards us, driven by the sound of the men beyond the ravine. One big male weaves in and out of the boulder field, and a man to my right fires and misses. Jóhannus takes aim and wings it, but the angle of the ground is too steep for a second shot. A tuft of hair floats into the air behind it, an ethereal thing like a dandelion seed head caught in the wind. The hare is not dead, and drags itself with drooping hind legs across the scree some way below. 'Can you get it?' Jóhannus shouts to me, and I scurry across the rough ground. Tórhallur is next in line and he too breaks off to chase the injured animal. 'It's OK,' I shout. 'I can do it!' I haven't a clear plan in my head but I'm racing as fast as I can, jumping from boulder to boulder to catch up with the animal and taking short sharp breaths of chilled air that I can feel going down into the back of my throat like iced water. Then, it's there at my feet just a metre or two away and still moving. Before I have time to think I reach down, unprepared for the high-pitched *eeegh-eeegh-eeegh* it lets out as my fingers close around its hind legs. It bucks and writhes, and I feel the sharp scratch of claws, drawing blood at the base of my thumb. This hare is larger, much heavier than the first two animals and without pausing to think about what to do, I swing it quickly through the air to dash its skull against the nearest boulder. Tórhallur is watching from a few metres away. 'OK?' he calls. 'Yes, OK,' I reply, and start the climb up to where Jóhannus waits on the ridgeline. I'm panting as I reach him, but warm from the effort. 'Here,' he says, pulling a length of nylon cord from his pocket. 'We'll make it a bit easier.' He fastens the cord around the hares' legs so that I can carry them over my shoulder like a bed roll on top of my back-pack. Each one is more than three kilograms and I notice the weight immediately as we continue walking. It's fine until one hare slips down and bangs against my right arm. Something sticky rubs against the back of my hand as I walk. I'm glad when we reach Mannaskarð, and it's time to rest.

More than thirty hares are piled together on a flat rock near to where the men are breaking open their snacks and pouring tea and coffee from flasks to warm themselves. There is a patchy blue sky to the north and east and the valley below is lit by a low sun. It burnishes a dozen glinting streams and a hundred rainwater pools making them shimmer like bubbles of mercury on the exposed basalt. There are no roads on this north-eastern part of the island, where open moors and steep valleys cover an area of over 130 square kilometres. In Vágar's distinctive dog's-head silhouette, we are running all over its upper jaw, and will finish the day in a cabin by the lake which forms its eye. Jóhannus says that I should stay by the hares and wait until the guns make a final sweep of the flank of Sandsdalur before tracking slightly north to Sveinssstiggjur, the edge of the escarpment that looks west along the northern coast. The wind is strong and there is rain coming now but I'm happy to stay and watch the drama unfold from above. The men aren't gone more than half an hour and then we resume the pattern of walking in line abreast. The ground drops away steeply, and we skirt outcrops of rock where hares can tuck themselves away in crevices. Few escape Jóhannus's eagle eye, and by the time we turn and head back towards the eastern edge of Tormanshagi, he has seven hares altogether. I now carry four but he has three in his back-pack and it doesn't seem to slow him down.

From the steep edge of Sveinsstíggjur, it is a long walk to a ridge overlooking Fjallavatn. Several rivers feed into this oblong body of water just a kilometre square, the second-largest lake in all Faroes. Tórbjørn says there are brown trout to be caught there. He has none of Jóhannus's natural bravado, and says little, but he moves very fast, never missing a shot when he spots a hare.

We stop for another brief rest at Flatnastíggjur, drinking the last of the tea and coffee. The smell of *sker-pikjøt* is all around. The light is dimmer now, and it is bitterly cold. Everyone looks tired, and someone has a log of how far we have walked on their phone pedometer. It's already twenty-four kilometres, and there's another ridge to cross before we can descend to the lakeside. Ahead Borgarheyggjur stands up from the land like a great stone nipple, and the men start to string out to encircle it. On the lakeward side, the ground drops sharply again so getting down to the path means a steep scramble. There are more hares on this side, and I see Tórbjørn, Tórhallur and Zacharis all make kills.

We reach the bothy as the light is turning the lake to polished chrome. We will sleep in Tórmanshúsið, a wooden cabin a few metres from the water's edge. Helgi's brother, Jákup Heri, is already there, and he comes out to greet us and inspect the hares. He has meaty hands and a ruddy complexion, weathered from years working on a fishing trawler in northern waters. He's come out to the lake especially to cook, having missed the hunt because he's been having trouble with his back. Jóhannus and Zach start stringing the hares up on a network of cords under the eaves of the hut. I count sixty-five in total, and later that night Jóhannus reports that it is the best tally being reported on the social-media hare-hunters group. A local biologist started the group as a citizen science project to gather data on the hare population, realising that the hunters were the best source of information. He has been able to record the total number of hares shot in each outfield, and annual totals range from 2500 to as many as 9000. Mountain hares reproduce quickly, with each female having three litters of two or three pups between February and September. Similar surveys in Scotland and Norway show that about a fifth of hares live beyond their first year, and it's clear that the majority hanging outside are young animals.

The hut is very simple, a tiny kitchen adjoining a small square sitting room with a dining table and, on the other side, a small bedroom with four bunk beds. The kitchen has no running water, so it has to be fetched from the lake. Cooking is on a bottle-fed gas stove, on which there is an enormous pan already bubbling away. On the floor beside the stove there is a bucket filled with potatoes, washed and ready for boiling. I smell fermented lamb, and Jákup Heri says he is preparing *kóka ræstkjøt*, neck, rump and legs of lamb for the nine of us. There will be *gularót* (carrots) and *kálrabirøtur* (kohlrabi) too.

The sitting room is crammed with large men and festooned with damp hiking socks and walking trousers suspended on string lines above a wood-burning stove. Cans of Slupp, the local beer, appear from the kitchen. From the windows there is a view across the lake, darkening now and empty.

'Tim, do you know you are in an English hut?' Tórbjørn asks later that night. 'Yes, this room we are in now was a radio shack built by the British during the war. After they left, my grandfather Ove brought it here to the lake, and over the years he added the kitchen and the bedroom on the sides.'

Here on Vágar we are not far from the airport, a critical strategic installation during the Second World War, and a base for many of the 8000 British servicemen who were stationed here after April 1940. Germany invaded Denmark on 9th April 1940, and Winston Churchill immediately announced that Faroes would be saved, partly due to their strategic importance, but also because, as he put in a characteristically rousing speech, 'the Faroese people show every disposition to receive us with warm regard. We shall shield the Faroe Islands from all the severities of war and establish ourselves there conveniently by sea and air until the moment comes when they will be handed back to Denmark liberated from the foul thraldom into which they have been plunged by German aggression.'

Four days after the German invasion of Denmark, the heavy cruiser HMS *Suffolk* deposited 193 Royal Marines in Tórshavn, led by a lieutenant colonel and accompanied by Frederick Mason, a twenty-six-year-old British consul, appointed by the Foreign Office. Mason became one of many British visitors to marry a local woman during the occupation. The British had their operational headquarters at Skansin fort in the capital. At the end of May, the Marines were replaced by a detachment of Lovat Scouts. They remained the principal regiment stationed in Faroes until 1942, when they were succeeded by the Cameronians.

The Scouts were originally formed as a Scottish sharp-shooter unit during the Boer War, and they included many men who had worked as gamekeepers and shepherds in civilian life, qualities which made them good marksmen and hardy enough to be comfortable patrolling the hills and valleys of Faroes. As the war progressed, they were joined by men from other regiments, including the Royal Artillery, the Pioneer Corps and the Royal Engineers, as well as naval and air force personnel. The RAF were a key part of the defence of Faroes, and it was RAF operations that led to the building of the first airport.

On Vágar only, because of the airfield, special identity cards were issued to the civilian population, and road traffic had to drive on the left-hand side – as it did in Britain. The threat from the enemy was real, and Faroes was attacked by German aeroplanes on several occasions. At sea, it's estimated that 210 Faroese sailors died due to enemy activity. The worst single loss of lives occurred when the unarmed fishing vessel *Nýggjaberg* out of Miðvágur was torpedoed south-east of Iceland on the night of 7th March 1942 by *U-701*. Sixteen of the twenty-one men on board came from Miðvágur, and in that village alone they left eight widows and thirty-two children. One of the villagers was the ship's master, fifty-eight-year-old Morten Mortensen, a father of twelve. Meanwhile, Georg Joensen, a skipper from Klaksvík, was awarded the MBE for single-handedly shooting down a German Heinkel that had strafed his fishing boat when he was sailing home to Faroes from Aberdeen. It's because of the contact with Britain during the war that my Faroese friends always delight in reminding me that they prefer Typhoo tea and Cadbury's chocolate to any other varieties. Each year, I am invited to a commemoration of Faroese Flag Day in London. The event marks the date (25th April) in 1940, when the BBC announced that Faroese vessels should fly the island flag, the *Merkið*, and not the Danish flag. The flag had been hoisted for the first time shortly after the British 'invasion' by Hans Mikkelsen, the skipper of the fishing boat *Eysturoy* that was sailing from Sørvágur to Aberdeen when it was intercepted by a British warship. The Royal Navy skipper asked if Mikkelsen had anything he could identify himself with other than the flag of a German occupied territory. Designed by Faroese students at Copenhagen University in 1919, the *Merkið* was not recognised by Denmark, but had been used unofficially at sporting events in Faroes, much to the Danish governor's irritation. It eventually became the official national flag for the islands when the Home Rule Act was passed in 1948.

During the Second World War, the catches made off Iceland by Faroese boats and landed at Scottish and northern English ports made up a significant portion of the fish reaching the country – crucial in allowing fish and chips to go unrationed. During the spring of 1941, Faroese vessels supplied an astonishing three-quarters of the fish landed. They often returned to Faroes carrying second-hand furniture to sell in the islands. Meanwhile, on land, there were around 170 marriages between the British troops and Faroese women, further strengthening links, especially with the Scottish communities which recruited men for the Lovat Scouts and the Cameronians.

In Tórmanshús there is no further talk of war. Slupp beer and schnapps are drunk and men speak of men's things: hunting and sheep, boats and weather, and women. Everyone chatters away in Faroese, but each man takes a turn at speaking to me in English and translating the gist of what's being said. Finally, there is washing-up to be done, and I make myself useful by filling the kettle with lake water to heat on the stove. I wade a little way out and my feet send out gentle ripples towards the dark centre of Fjallavatn. The air is cold, and lapping water echoes in the cold night air. When I come back inside, everyone laughs because Jóhannus has taken a photograph of me on his phone. The image is blurred, and they say it is not me in the grey Faroes wool *undirtroyggja* in the lake, but one of the hill people, the *huldufólk*, who inhabit the outfield and have the power to make men disappear. The wood stove throws out enormous heat and the rich smells of drying wool and the remnants of Jákup Heri's mutton stew combine in a cosy fug. When the time comes for sleep, each man takes a free bunk and the room soon thrums with the sound of snoring. The wind puffs in strong rhythmic bursts against the window overlooking the lake towards the west. The physical exertion of the long day on the mountain has left me utterly relaxed. I realise that this alternative life on these stormy rocks has brought with it a rediscovery of my sense of self, spawning the strongest sense of homecoming.

12

Nest

Spring, punctuated by heavy rain and winds, is slowly moving across Vágar. People have begun sowing potatoes, and I realise it is almost two months since St Patrick's Day – that was when my grandfather always told me we should dig the ground. I was ten when I was given my own growing patch at the end of the garden and he taught me how to sift the soil with an ancient griddle to clear it of weeds and stones before planting. I remember how tenderly he always picked out the worms and placed them back in the earth. Then there was the long wait and the excitement of watching the first shoots appear above the ground. After school each day, I raced home to measure how much higher the plants had grown. I remember the thrill of reaping the crop in September, something to look forward to after being trapped all day indoors. Digging them up, washing off the soil and giving the shiny tubers to my mother to boil felt like a grand achievement. In Miðvágur, I join friends on a hillside above the village as they sow this year's seed potatoes. We look down towards the narrow harbour with its breakwater and across the sea towards the high forbidding end of Koltur. There is a fresh breeze coming from the west and a threat of rain.

Potatoes are planted using the 'lazy bed' system, a technique common in Ireland and imported to Faroes from the Hebrides in the early twentieth century. Rather than digging a deep trench for planting, a sharp spade is use to cut parallel pairs of shallow 'tram lines' into the sod, and seed potatoes are placed in a neat row on the grass between two of the cuts. On alternate rows, the topsoil is then shaved off in squares to a depth of a couple of inches, making a neat flap of earth which is then flipped over onto the potato seedling, grass side down. Then a handful of fertiliser (once upon a time just a lump of seaweed or some fish heads) is added to the seedling, and it is left to grow, avoiding the need for deep digging, and providing better drainage. It's a technique especially suited to poor wet soil and helps protect the seedlings from frost. The sod makes a tearing sound like an old cotton dishcloth being ripped in half. My friends laugh when I place my foot on the top of the shovel blade for extra purchase as I shave off the turf. 'Look! He does it like a girl!' Apparently, a Faroese man manages to dig with his arms alone. Luckily, the rain comes and we stop before I have to admit to being tired. But not too tired to go and see if the ravens have come back to last year's nest. By the time I reach the gorge, the rain has eased off and the damp ground deadens the sound of my approach.

The fulmars are back in their pairs, huddled breast to breast and rubbing their beaks together. They chatter raucously when I appear but soon settle down to preening and chattering as they keep jealous guard of the prime grassy perches on the cliff. They mate clumsily and for several minutes at a time. The hills are greening again, and the first colonies of rock cress are sending tiny white flowers up from crevices in the basalt close to the shore.

The ravens' nest has survived the winter and been fortified with new twigs and bones. The bowl is freshly lined with down. I have seen the adult birds in the distance once or twice, but today there is one on the nest, almost certainly the female. With the wind from the south, she doesn't hear me coming until I'm at the edge of the ravine, crawling the last ten metres so as not to loom above the skyline. For a few seconds she does not notice my presence, but then she opens her wings and with a couple of beats is out and flying down the gorge towards the open sea. I will stay just a few minutes, so as not to disturb her for too long.

This year's chicks are freshly hatched. Bald and blind, their large bruise-blue eyes show through closed lids. There are cottonball patches of fine down on their backs but they are otherwise almost naked. Small heads move in a jerky, uncoordinated way with mouths stretched wide to show that bright pink interior. Their beaks, more broadly triangular than in the older birds, open and close like one of those origami fortune-telling games children make out of paper, the one where four folded cones meet in the middle and you pick a number to read what lies underneath. The fortunes of these newborn ravens are uncertain. But the low *krorking* call of the adults is echoing across the water as I scan the surface with my binoculars. They have reunited in the air and are flying in formation towards the safety of the ridge from where they will spy on me. The dark birds take turns to circle the hillside above the ravine as I rise from my viewpoint. This is their place again and they must be left to rear their new chicks on the shadowy cliffs. In a few months, a new generation of ravens will ride the wild Atlantic wind.

Acknowledgements

This book could not have been written without the help of my many friends in the Faroe Islands. Hospitality, kindness and tireless patience in answering questions from a curious *onglendingur* were offered with a generosity of spirit which, in all of my travels, I have met nowhere else on earth. I must thank Stan Abbott for my very first opportunity to visit the islands, and for introducing me to several people who have been crucial to my research and travels around the archipelago, beginning with the ever generous Johannes Jensen. My continuing journalism about Faroes has been possible through the assistance of Guðrið Højgaard and her team at Visit Faroe Islands, with special thanks to Súsanna Sørensen for her willingness to vouch for me with so many people over the years. Levi Hanssen must take credit for introducing me to Jóhannus Hansen, an extraordinary guide, mountaineer, shepherd and outdoorsman willing to tutor me in the fine details of Faroese livestock and wildlife. For including me in their family meals and an always warm welcome in their home, I thank Dánial Petur and Lisa Hansen on Vágar, and to Vilhelm Hansen many thanks are due for linguistic advice and safe travels at sea.

In Tórshavn, I must single out Dr Pál Weihe and Julianna Klett of *Listafelag Føroya*, whose generosity allowed me to benefit from the legacy of the artist Janus Kamban. Pál is also renowned for his expertise in epidemiological research into pilot whale contaminants in his role as head of the Faroe Islands' Department of Occupational Medicine and Public Health. Pilot whale biology was provided by Bjarni Mikkelsen from the Faroes Museum of Natural History, while mountain hare facts came courtesy of research by Eyðfinn Magnussen at Faroe Islands University.

On Mykines, I am grateful to Esbern í Eyðansstovu and Katrina Johannesen. Many others from that small community allowed me to observe and contribute in a small way to catching sheep, including Tummas and Maja Henriksen. Tórbjørn Poulsen offered generous hospitality at Fjallavatn more than once, and kept me safe in the mountains on Vágar and Mykines. In Miðvágur, thanks go to Marit Johansdóttir Magnussen and her brother Napolion Jóhansson Magnussen for tuition in potato planting and traditional rowing. Johann Ludvík Laksafoss provided valued historical knowledge. And, close by, thanks for a memorable meal of sheep's heads, fresh potatoes, milk and gin must go to Jákup Pauli í Eyðansstovu. Advice on the mysteries of traditional Faroese food was gratefully received from Professor Jóan Pauli Joensen and Jógvan Páll Fjallsbak – head of microbiology at the Food and Veterinary agency. More specific dietary delights were offered in many Faroese homes, and by the stratospherically talented chef Poul Andrias Ziska and his team at Koks. Food cannot be mentioned without acknowledging the cooking skills of Jákup Heri Leonson on Mykines and at Fjallavatn. Political and historic insights were provided over several years by the redoubtable Magni Arge, and the joy of aerial views of the archipelago were courtesy of Captain Jón Falkvard.

I have been exceptionally privileged to pay several visits to the cosiest farmhouse in the world on Stóra Dímun, and be welcomed and befriended by Eva úr Dímun and Jógvan Jón Petersen, Janus úr Dímun and his wife Erla, and all of their respective children. On Skúvoy, Tummas Frank Joensen, his wife Elisabeth and son Jón made me very welcome, as did Bjørn and Lúkka Patursson on Koltur. Other members of the extended Patursson clan also deserve thanks – especially Jóannes Patursson, who farms at Kirkjubøur, and Tjóðhild Patursson on Nólsoy. Further north, on Viðoy, I must recognise Tóri Simonsen for skilful seamanship and fowling advice. For help and friendship (and a woolly hat) on Mykines and Sandoy, I thank Benjámin Lydersen. During egg-collecting season on Sandoy, I was made welcome by Bjarki Henriksen and his extended family.

Another book could be written about the pervasiveness of music in Faroe Islands, and I have been lucky to hear so many exceptional performers from that world through the kindness of Jón Tyril, Kristian Blak and Sharon Weiss among others. Natural history expertise has been gratefully received from 'the bird man of Nólsoy', Jens-Kjeld Jensen, and much additional botanical wisdom from his wife Marita Gulklett. Thanks for sharing their ornithological knowledge on storm petrels and ravens in particular also goes to Jógvan Thomsen, Abraham Mikladal and

Hein Van Grouw (at the Natural History Museum at Tring).

I must also thank Áki Johansen, the Faroese government representative in London, and his colleague Hugo Lamhauge Hansen for welcoming me over several years to Flag Day commemorations and other events.

In Faroes, Zakarias Wang offered meticulous linguistic advice (any mistakes in the text are mine) and I must also thank Urd Johannesen, Sissal Kampmann and Heiðrik á Heygum for their literary-minded encouragement. Many other people have given me their time generously, providing meals and accommodation on so many visits, including protracted hospitality and shelter from Óluva Zachariasen and Eyðun Vestergaard Hjaltalin and Christel Christopherson. *Hjartans tøkk til tykkum øll.*

Writing this book has been made significantly easier through the provision of a Royal Literary Fund Fellowship at Exeter College, University of Oxford. I thank the Rector, Professor Sir Rick Trainor, and all of the staff and Fellows at the college for making me so welcome during my stay. Thanks, as always, go to my long-standing literary agent, Natasha Fairweather at Rogers, Coleridge and White.

Selected Reading

Atkinson, George Clayton *Journal of an Expedition to the Feroe & Westman Islands and Iceland, 1833*, Bewick-Beaufort Press, 1989

Barnes, Tony Major *The Faroe Islands Force 1940-45*, Salisbury, 2017

Bengtson, S.A. et al *Dorete – her book; being a tribute to Dorete Bloch and to Faroese nature*, Faroes University Press, Tórshavn 2010

Bjørk, E.A. *Færøsk bygderet*, Tórshavn, 1956

Debes, Lucas Jacobson *Faeroe, & Foeroa Reserata: That is a Description of the Islands and Inhabitants of Foeroa: Being Seventeen Islands subject to the King of Denmark, lying under 62 deg. 10 min. of North Latitude*, London, 1676

Djernes, M. *Aircraft Crash on the Island of Mikenes* (sic) Faroes, Proc. Int. Congress on Disaster Medicine, Springer-Verlag, Mainz, 1977

Faulkes, Anthony (trans) *Færeyinga Saga*, Thorisdal, Dundee 2016

Feilden, H.W. *Birds of the Faroe Islands*, Zoologist (Journal), 1872

Foote, P.G. *On the Saga of the Faroe Islanders*, Inaugural Lecture at UCL, 1964

Freethy, Ron *Auks: An Ornithologist's Guide*, Blandford Press, Poole, 1987

Harris, George Herbert *The Faroe Islands*, Cornish Bros., Birmingham, 1927

Ingólfsson, Aðalsteinn *Mikines*, Nesútgáfan, Reykjavik, 2006

Jackson, Anthony *The Faroes: The Faraway Islands*, Robert Hale, London, 1991

Jacobsen, Jørgen-Frantz *Barbara*, (trans. W. Glyn Jones), Dedalus, UK, 2013

Joensen, Jóan Pauli *Pilot Whaling in the Faroe Islands*, Faroe University Press, Tórshavn, 2009

Joensen, Jóan Pauli *Traditional Faroese Food Culture*, Faroe University Press, Tórshavn, 2016

Hammer, Sjúður et al *Færøsk Trækfugleatlas*, Faroe University Press, Tórshavn, 2014

Kerins, Séan *A Thousand Years of Whaling*, CCI Press, Edmonton, 2010

Landt, G. *A Description of the Feroe Islands* (trans) Longman, London, 1810

Linklater, Eric *The Dark of Summer*, Canongate, Edinburgh, 1991

Matras, Christian *Seydabrævid*, Foroya Fródskaparfelag, Tórshavn, 1971

Press, Muriel A.C. *The Saga of the Faroe Islanders*, J.M. Dent, London, 1934

Murray, Donald S. *The Guga Hunters*, Birlinn, Edinburgh, 2015

Nicol, James *An Historical and Descriptive Account of Iceland, Greenland and the Faroe Islands: with illustrations of their natural history*, Oliver & Boyd, Edinburgh, 1840

Nordgate, Sydney *'Kanska' or The Land of Maybe,* Jakobsens, Tórshavn, 1943

Painter, K. Robert, *Faroe-Islander Saga*, McFarland, North Carolina, 2016

Pálsson, Hermann (trans) *The Book of Settlements* (*Landnámabók*), University of Manitoba Press, Winnipeg, 2006

Powell, F. York (trans) *The Saga of Thrond of Gate*, D Nutt, London, 1896

Proctor, James, *Faroe Islands*, Bradt, Chesham, 2016

Rasmussen, Jóannes, *Geology of the Faeroe Islands*, Reitzel, Copenhagen, 1970

Schei, Liv Kjørsvik & Moberg, Gunnie, *The Faroe Islands*, Birlinn, Edinburgh, 2003

Svanberg, Ingvar *Ræstur fiskur: air-dried fermented fish the Faroese way*, Journal of Ethnobiology and Ethnomedicine, Springer Nature, 2015

Szabo, Vicki Ellen, *Monstrous Fishes and the Mead Dark Sea*, Brill, Leiden, 2007

Taylor, Elizabeth, *The Far Islands and Other Cold Places*, Pogo Press, 1997

West, John F. *Faroe: the emergence of a nation*, C. Hurst & Co., London, 1972

West, John F. *The History of the Faroe Islands*, 1709-1816, Reitzel, Copenhagen, 1985

Williamson, Kenneth, *The Atlantic Islands*, Collins, London, 1948

Wylie, Jonathan & Margolin, David *The Ring of Dancers*, University of Pennsylvania Press, Philadelphia 1981

Young, G.V.C. *From the Vikings to the Reformation: A Chronicle of the Faroe Islands up to 1538*, Shearwater Press, Isle of Man, 1979

Tim Ecott is a former BBC World Service staff correspondent. He has worked widely in Africa and the Indian Ocean. He writes documentaries for radio and screen and non-fiction, drawing heavily on his fondness for the natural world. His books include: *Neutral Buoyancy* (Penguin), *Vanilla: Travels in search of the luscious substance* (Penguin), *Stealing Water* (Sceptre) and *The Story of Seychelles* (Outer Island Books).